DOGS OF DREAMTIME

DOGS OF DREAMTIME

A STORY ABOUT SECOND CHANCES
AND THE POWER OF LOVE

BY KAREN SHANLEY

THE LYONS PRESS
Guilford, Connecticut

An imprint of The Globe Pequot Press

Copyright © 2005 by Karen Shanley

First Lyons Press paperback edition, 2007

ALL RIGHTS RESERVED. No part of this book may be reproduced or transmitted in any form by any means, electronic or mechanical, including photocopying and recording, or by any information storage and retrieval system, except as may be expressly permitted in writing from the publisher. Requests for permission should be addressed to The Lyons Press, Attn: Rights and Permissions Department, P.O. Box 480, Guilford, CT 06437.

The Lyons Press is an imprint of The Globe Pequot Press.

10 9 8 7 6 5 4 3

Printed in the United States of America

Designed by Sheryl P. Kober

ISBN-13: 978-1-59221-085-8

The Library of Congress has previously cataloged an earlier (hardcover) edition as follows:

Shanley, Karen.
    Dogs of dreamtime : a story about second chances and the power of love / by Karen Shanley.
        p. cm.
    ISBN 1-59228-820-0 (trade cloth)
    1. Dogs—United States—Anecdotes. 2. Shanley, Karen. 3. Women dog owners—United States—Anecdotes. 4. Human-animal relationships—United States—Anecdotes. I. Title.
SF426.2.S49 2005
                                                                    2005022248

This one's for you, Magic.

CONTENTS

O

The Coyotes Call

THEIR BANSHEE WAILS reached through my dreams and dragged me back. Instinctively, my eyes flickered open. Frozen still, hardly breathing, I cocked my head slightly off the pillow trying to pinpoint their location. From the proximity of their cries, I calculated they were within a hundred feet of the house. Awake now, on full red alert, heart thumping, my eyes anxiously swept the room to find my three-year-old Australian Shepherd, Kiera. Relieved, I saw that she lay safely by the foot of the bed, lost in her own dreams, her legs twitching in a truncated trot. She hadn't heard them.

I quietly rushed to lock the bedroom door so that Kiera couldn't escape and go after them through the dog door. This had become an all-too-familiar late-night ritual. As I returned to bed, she groggily looked up at me. I whispered, "Not tonight, my girl," and reached down to stroke her mohair-soft black-and-white fur before slipping soundlessly back under the covers next to my still-sleeping husband. The clock showed a little past midnight.

For the past few years, these coyotes had taken to showing up nights and howling at the edges of our property just as major events were about to unfold. Their unsettling songs alternated between haunting ballads and uncanny impersonations of trilling Greek women mourning their dead. They weaved in and out of my waking and sleeping life.

I'd come to see them as harbingers, their appearances fore-shadowing critical turning points. What were they telling me now? I'd already lost more than I could bear to lose. There had been tremendous love but even greater sorrow. If there was more coming, I was afraid I'd break wide open and the most essential parts of me would begin leaking out.

I was wide awake now. Wired, my mind riffled through a clutter of images—every one of them crammed with edgy emotions. A lone coyote howled, as if to punctuate my thoughts.

This pack of coyotes had also beaten paths through the perimeters of our property during the day. One morning, I'd watched a mother move warily across the fields, with her young pups all bunched up, tumbling along behind her. Another time, I'd been startled by a long-legged gray standing motionless only a few feet away, staring out silently from the camouflage of the thick underbrush. There was the day, too, when I'd studied a mangy dead one at the end of our road. A car had hit her. And then there was the stately and rather large one who was drinking from our pond, within twenty paces of me. He'd considered me for several long seconds through tourmaline-colored eyes before he slipped into the nearby woods. For animals that were supposed to be elusive, I was seeing an awful lot of them.

○

The coyotes started up again in a riot of barks, yips, and screams. This time, Kiera, though exhausted from her evening run with my husband, Andrew, was quivering at attention. Her rocketlike readiness for flight was contagious, setting off my adrenaline. She blasted to the bedroom door and tried to turn the knob with her paws. Discovering she'd been foiled, she rico-cheted back to the open window, pressing her nose against the screen, fervently sniffing at the cool September night air. She began to pace, snort, and whine.

Watching her brain at work never lost its fascination—this dog of mine, escape artist extraordinaire. She could open any door not locked, climb over any barrier, and crawl through nearly any space, defying the laws of physics and gravity. Her intelligence shone as brightly as her coat.

When all her usual tricks failed, she leapt up and pawed at me, nudging under my arm with her nose, as though she'd convinced herself that she could single-handedly lift me out of bed and will me to set her free.

She couldn't help her conflicting urges any more than I could help mine. She wanted to fly out the door after the coyotes. She wanted to guard, herd, and protect. She wanted to chase them off. I wondered, too, if there wasn't some part of her that wanted to run free with them. I couldn't help but wonder if given the chance—really given the chance—this urge ultimately would drive her. As much as her heart was mine, as much as every instinctive nerve in her body was wired to stay by me and protect, I wondered if the lure of the pack called to something even deeper in her—a sense of tribe, her tribe.

For the moment, the ruckus died down again. Kiera, still electric with energy, nuzzled me as if asking me to help her wick away the excess. I got down on the floor and pulled her into my arms. I buried my face in her scruff and breathed in deeply the grassy smell of her fur. I scratched under her chest and murmured in her ear. I could feel her body begin to relax. I was as much her touchstone as she was mine. I stretched myself out along the length of her. She pushed her rump back into the curve of my body and exhaled a contented little groan. It wouldn't be long before she'd be back in a deep sleep.

As I absentmindedly stroked her side, I tried to think back to when it all began. To the time when I'd started feeling that somehow I was at the wrong end of a collision of circumstances.

It was about three years before, when I went from having

no dogs to three dogs in the span of four months. Each dog brought challenges and gifts. First came Kiera and her sibling Molly. Then Molly unwittingly became the agent for Magic's unplanned arrival. Just before Magic came, the coyotes made their first appearance.

These were some intense dog days, literally and figuratively. I couldn't have known then how the confluence of these comings and goings would play out. I couldn't have known, either, how my love for these dogs would so irrevocably change my life.

I thought back to how that was also the time when Andrew decided he wanted out of a very successful business partnership. He wanted his freedom badly enough to risk walking away and starting over from scratch. Even though I had concerns, I couldn't stand in the way of something so essential. He also needed me to help him run his new advertising business, so I shoved my fears as far down into my unconscious as I could pack them, and chose instead to bank on our combined talents and capacity for hard work to carry us through.

By itself, this tremor might have passed without much notice. But in the span of the previous few years, I'd given birth to my daughter, Caitlin, and had also closed my own lucrative consulting business so I could be a forty-one-year-old stay-at-home mom. It was only a few weeks after Caitlin's birth that the succession of deaths began. Between us, Andrew and I lost three parents, two close relatives, a dear friend, and four beloved animals. There was barely a chance to recover from one death before the next one hit.

While I kept a good game face—I could list these events to anyone who might inquire with all the detachment of someone ticking off a grocery list—the truth of the matter was that it was taking every ounce of my energy not to get sucked into a black hole. I felt overwhelmed and lost. It had been too much change. Too much loss. I couldn't get my bearings. I had never been in this place before, and it scared me. I'd always considered myself a strong person, the Rock of Gibraltar. But I didn't feel strong anymore. I just felt like crying.

As I lay there holding Kiera, reviewing the events that had occurred since she'd come into my life, I thought about how I'd become so distressingly aware of the gulf between my need for my dogs, the outdoors, the craving for what's real and immediate, against what had become the contrasting drudgery of daily life, so full of so many things I didn't care about, and so few that I did.

It wasn't that I'd lost sight that I considered myself lucky. I was daily nourished by my bond with Andrew. We shared a love and friendship that was deep and clean. I adored Caitlin, little spitfire that she was. I was thankful for the close relationships I had with my two wonderful stepsons, Colin and McLean, of whom I was very proud. And, incredibly, I still had Kiera. It was because of these loves that I didn't let myself untie the string and float away on the wisps of any whispering breeze.

Still, I knew I had to do something. I had to figure out what it had all meant to me; I had to make some kind of sense out of everything that had happened. I also had to start looking at what was right in front of me. More trouble was brewing. I'd already witnessed the early signs. Kiera was starting to pick up where Magic had left off. It was beginning to look like déjà vu all over again. I had to figure out what facing this next struggle meant to me. God knows, the stakes had become unbearably high.

There are different kinds of love and different kinds of things that nourish who we are. It was obvious to me that all of my dogs had provided me with a kind of love and sustenance that only they could. But Kiera went beyond even that. What was it about Kiera? Why had it been so absolutely necessary that I try to find her, no matter how crazy it all seemed? It was as though an unfathomable force linked the two of us together. To say that it was as simple as Kiera and I belonged together wouldn't begin to touch what it was—this thing that made me feel that I wouldn't be able to go on without her. It was so powerful.

When Magic died, something got lost. Something that felt very profound—a connection, a love, his being. But if something happened to Kiera . . . If I lost Kiera, I'd feel that I'd lost a piece of my soul.

○

My questions remained unanswered that night as I finally let go of Kiera and got back into bed, searching for sleep again. It wouldn't be until much later that I'd learn what the coyotes were trying to tell me. That last call of the coyotes was a signal that my journey with my dogs was about to come full circle. I was about to be offered a chance at redemption. But with one condition: I'd have to find a way to recapture my faith. My faith in life itself. To let myself believe once again that the possibility for redemption existed.

At the beginning, I didn't know any of this.

I knew only that, with the loss of my father as my steadying guide through life, I needed to find myself another teacher— someone who would challenge me to climb up and out from under the dust and debris, so that I could begin to see with crystal clarity again.

There's the saying, "When the student is ready, the teacher appears." My teachers appeared in force. Only I never would have guessed that they'd be who they were, and serve up the lessons they brought.

As with any spiritual journey, and this was a spiritual journey, some getting lost was necessary before I could be found. Ultimately, I would come to understand why each one of my dogs had been sent to me, and the role they played in helping me to find myself.

In the end, I would win back that crystal clarity, but I'd have to cross the River Styx to get it.

Let me take you back to where it all began, three years ago.

DOGS OF DREAMTIME

○

PART ONE
Kiera

CHAPTER 1

Searching for the Dalai Lama

SHE WAS JUST sitting there, cool as a cucumber, staring right up at me. She was so still, I wasn't sure she was real. As I inched forward for a closer look, I could see her bright eyes blink and her body vibrate with excitement. She was exceedingly happy to see that I'd come, but she was more concerned with making sure I got a real good look at her, and that I burned the picture into my brain. Until I did, she was unwilling to move. I can't tell you how I knew this exactly; it was something in the way she locked her eyes onto mine. So I took in as much of her as I could and committed it to memory.

No more than eight weeks old, with round puppy tummy, she was obsidian black, with fluffy white shawl around neck and chest. She had a white muzzle, with a blaze traveling up and over the top of her head, meeting up with white scruff between shoulders. Four white socks. Little tan eyebrows. No tail.

As I was busy soaking in every detail, I could have sworn I heard her say, "I've come back to be with you."

This startled me so much that I woke up.

The dream had been so vivid and so real that, for a moment, I wasn't sure where I was. Could it be possible . . . ?

○

My beloved Sheltie, Kiera, at eleven years, had died from a brain tumor not quite one year before. She'd been my unswerving friend and safehold through some of the most significant changes in my life. She'd seen me through changes in relationship, career, and geographic location, as well as the milestones of marriage, birth, and death. Her presence had always had the effect of steadying me in a way that no other could. I tried to offer her as much when it came time for me to let her go.

I'd prayed that I would know when that day was, and, mercifully, my prayers were answered. It came on a calm fall morning, shortly after we'd exhausted all the treatments available. Disoriented and unbalanced, Kiera could no longer stand up. She couldn't eat. She wouldn't drink. I called the vet. He agreed to come to our house so she could die peacefully in my arms, in her home. I cradled her, whispering gently, telling her over and over how much I loved her, stroking and kissing her beautiful face, my tears staining her fur, until she took her last breath.

After the vet left, I sat holding her for a long while, unwilling to give up the feel of her in my arms. After some time, Andrew gently helped me take the next step. He went and got the blanket I'd planned to wrap her in. It was her favorite blanket, one that I'd made for her when she was a puppy. Then we buried her under the shade of an arching ash tree by my garden.

The ache from her absence was still very much with me. I'd reconciled myself to remaining dogless. Kiera had been such an exceptional companion that I was afraid any other dog would always suffer from the comparison.

That Kiera would come back to solve this problem for me would be just like her. The very notion had me shaking my head and chuckling out loud. Still, this really would be too fantastic to be true—even for my wonder dog.

Mesmerized by this thought, I moved trancelike around the kitchen that morning, while some other part of me got my four-year-old daughter's breakfast ready. Andrew sat with the morning paper in one hand and a cup of coffee in the other. Caitlin, a blend of the both of us, having my sandy blond hair and curved mouth, and Andrew's sparkling blue eyes and gangly arms and legs, wasn't used to all this quiet. She piped up, "I had a funny dream last night, Mom."

Snapped out of my reverie, I answered, "You did? What was it?"

We're a family of prolific dreamers, and sharing them at breakfast has become something of a tradition at our house. It's a way for us to start the day feeling more settled and connected.

As Cait began her recollection, Andrew put down his paper to give her his full attention.

She began, "Well, I was walking in the woods behind our house and . . ."

It was another bear dream.

I'd been trying to get Cait to enjoy hiking in the woods with me. There was a beautiful, gently rolling path that meandered around a lake not far from my mother's house a couple of hours north of us in the Adirondacks. I'd made the mistake of forcing the issue one day, even after my normally spunky daughter had refused several times. She reluctantly came along with me, and, though we saw no wildlife to speak of, she finished the walk somehow associating woods with a fear of bears. She'd spent many dreams working this out. In this dream, the bear had turned out to be a friend, so that was progress.

After Cait shared her dream, Andrew looked over to me and asked, "So, Mom, any dreams last night?" They both waited expectantly.

"Uh, no . . . ," I lied, "I don't remember any."

I wasn't ready to share this particular dream for a couple of reasons. It wasn't that I thought Andrew would dismiss my dream as strange or silly—on the contrary, after all these years, he'd gotten used to more than the occasional dream of mine somehow managing to drop into reality. It was just that the subject of animals in our household was always a loaded one. I was a dyed-in-the-wool animal lover. Andrew was not.

Whenever I'd had animals in my life, they'd always consumed a considerable amount of my attention and love—Andrew might say an inordinate amount. Having gone through a spate of human and animal losses within the last few years, I knew that Andrew would have two reactions to my dream. He hated the thought of seeing me set myself up for more loss, even if it was a loss that was more than likely at least a decade away. And he was enjoying the benefits of an animal-free home—no hair on clothes, no tripping over furry bodies, no worrying about when we had to get back home or how much dog exercise needed to be fit in.

So, even if there was a remote basis to my dream, even if Kiera *had* found a way to come back, Andrew wouldn't be inclined to want any part of it. He'd be apt to say this was just as likely brought on by my recent research into dog breeds. (I'd been trying to help a friend find a dog who would make a good buddy for her young daughter. This little girl was paralyzed from the neck down and spent her days in a wheelchair.) And I'd have to allow that this analysis could be true.

I'd spent the last couple of weeks investigating some breeds that my vet had recommended. His list of suggestions had included Border Terriers, Australian Shepherds, and German Shepherds. I was already familiar with German Shepherds, as almost everyone is. And my mother had quite a wonderful old German Shepherd girl, of whom I was very fond. I'd never heard of the other two breeds, so I hit the Internet to get educated. Border Terriers looked kind of like "Benji" dogs, with little otter-shaped heads. They were on the smallish side of a medium build, and did what terriers do very well—hunt rodents, foxes, et al. Australian Shepherds, or "Aussies," basically looked like

Border Collies on steroids, without tails. They were medium-sized herding dogs. What all three breeds had in common was that they were all very intelligent, loyal, working dogs needing lots of exercise and stimulation to be happy.

Given the limited information I'd relayed to my vet, I could see why he'd suggested these breeds. I had emphasized the guarding and companion qualities that my friend wanted for her daughter. But as I delved deeper into learning about all these dogs, I became concerned that none of them would be a good fit for first-time dog owners. These were all dogs who would go squirrelly after a while just lying around keeping an eye on a little girl who wouldn't even be able to throw a ball for them. I also knew it was extremely unlikely that anyone else in her home would have the time to adequately exercise such high-octane animals.

My friend eventually wound up with a very sweet little Bichon Frise.

I wound up with an acute case of "Aussie-itis."

I'd become totally smitten. I'd always had herding dogs, and had become hooked on their intelligence and character. I'd had a long-standing love affair with Border Collies but was discouraged from getting one by a dog-loving friend who'd had several. Not one to mince words, she put it this way: Unless I was willing to get some sheep, too, I should do them a favor and leave them alone. These were dogs who needed a job. From what I could gather, Aussies, while similar to Border Collies in many ways, appeared to be a little less intense (or, as my friend would bluntly suggest, less inclined to be neurotic). Anyway, if I were ever in the market for another dog, I knew what breed it would be.

Taking all of these recent developments into account, I knew that Andrew's response would be a flat "No," so there was no point in going there. I tried to put the idea right out of my head.

And I did.

Until a few nights later, when a remarkably similar dream played itself out. The same little Aussie puppy sat stock-still again, looking up at me. This time, I sat down next to her, to pet her. She couldn't contain herself any longer; she bounded up into my arms and slathered me with puppy kisses. I held her close and relished the wonderful smell of her puppy breath.

Again, she announced—quite clearly this time—that she'd come back for me. Again, I awoke with a start. Lying there, I didn't know whether to laugh or cry. This was all too much to contemplate.

A few more days passed, and with each new day I found it harder and harder to get her out of my head. I had this over-powering sensation that she was with me everywhere I went. It occurred to me that if I was going to try to find her, she was already around eight weeks old. That meant I'd have a couple of weeks at most to track her down before she might be sold to any buyer who happened to be in the market for an Australian Shepherd female pup. My stomach knotted up at the thought of her going to someone else's home. I felt an uncomfortable urgency growing.

I was nervous about talking to Andrew about these dreams. It wasn't that he was unreasonable or unfeeling. It was just that I didn't want to force another dog on him when he felt that he was finally home free. There was so much about having a dog that had been a struggle for him, even though he had come to dearly love Kiera before she died, and even though he mourned her death nearly as deeply as I did. I also knew how much Andrew loved me, and how much he'd try to do anything for me if he thought it was something I really needed. Weighing it all out, I decided I'd have a better-than-even chance if he was made aware of how much this meant to me.

At the first quiet moment, I decided to bring it up. After we'd gotten Cait to sleep one evening, we sat down in the living room. Our way of unwinding has always been to sit and talk at the end of the day.

The conversation began with discussing a potentially big client with whom we'd just acquired a hard-won meeting. On that happy note, I segued into my "exciting" news.

"Boy, have I been having some really weird dreams lately," I began.

"What are they?" Andrew asked.

"Well, Kiera's come back . . ."

The words hung in the air.

The mood in the room instantly changed. Andrew looked at me, not quite knowing what to say.

I hurriedly went on to explain that I'd been having these dreams where Kiera made it clear that she fully expected me to come and find her. It was also clear that it didn't occur to her that I might fail. I hoped to get Andrew to see that I couldn't let her down; I couldn't lose her if she really had come back for me.

He didn't even comment on the strangeness of the dreams, or what they might mean. He just said, "Please, I can't do another dog."

"But—"

"I don't want any more dogs. I like our life the way it is. Besides, even if I said yes, what would be the odds that you could find her? If she has come back, she could be anywhere in the country."

Without actually coming right out and saying the whole idea was ludicrous, Andrew had landed a one–two punch. Realistically, I hadn't considered what the search might mean. And I really did respect Andrew's feelings. I really didn't want to make our lives more complicated. But this was a no-win situation: One of us was going to be unhappy no matter what happened.

I conceded Round One. The conversation turned to other subjects.

The next night, she came again. This time I could see that she was in some kind of farmlike setting with several other puppies and dogs. I awoke thinking this would help rule out some breeders. But it would still be an incredible long shot, notwithstanding this whole idea of her reincarnating to be with me again in the first place. I was beginning to feel a little nutty.

Even so, I couldn't stop myself and began furtively looking up breeders on the Web. I started with a local search, assuming that if Kiera had gone to the trouble of figuring out how to come back, she wouldn't choose someplace thousands of miles away. She'd want to land as close to me as she could—or so I specu- lated. Then it would be a matter of finding breeders who had puppies around eight weeks old, specifically one black-and- white female puppy.

Christmas was less than a week away. I was normally much more organized about the holidays, but I was hopelessly far be- hind this year. The new business was still front and center, con- suming all our efforts. I wasn't one to go in for the commercialism of the season anyway, but I always liked to take some time to find a few really thoughtful gifts. As it was, by ne- cessity, presents would be sparse this year. Andrew and I had agreed not to get each other anything. So, amid the encroaching holiday chaos, my desire to persuade Andrew about Kiera, and my attempts to find her, were put on the back burner.

○

Christmas morning rolled around. Colin had arrived home from his freshman year at college earlier in the week. Both he and McLean, a junior in high school, were still asleep upstairs. Cait had used up every ounce of restraint she could muster. It was nine o'clock; she had been up since six. Andrew finally gave her the go-ahead to wake her brothers. She jumped on each of their beds until she was sure they'd be incapable of falling back to sleep. Her job done, she raced back downstairs and began opening presents.

By late morning, the stockings had been emptied, and the bottom of the tree was looking pretty bare. There had been a few surprises and much to be thankful for. The kids were organizing their stuff into neat little piles. I was about to go start breakfast when Andrew motioned to me and took out a white envelope from his back pocket.

As he handed it to me, I shot him an irritated look that said: *We promised not to exchange anything . . . We can't afford to exchange anything . . . I kept my end of the bargain and didn't get you anything . . . There's nothing I want or need . . .*

The card contained three words: "Go find her." There was a blank check inside.

The magnitude of his gesture opened the floodgates. I broke down and wept.

○

After everyone had gone to bed, I burned the midnight oil, compiling my hit list of breeders. I started calling the next morning.

○

Breeder #1: Long Island, New York. "We have a few championship dogs but we don't have any puppies right now. We'll be having a litter in June. I could reserve a female for you, and you'd have her by August."

I crossed her off the list. One down, six to go.

○

Breeder #2: Two hours north. "Yes, we have some puppies."

"Do you have any females?"

"Yes, we have two. One is a blue merle," she announced, as though she thought that should be reason enough to take a drive.

"Great. When would it be convenient for me to come and see them?" I asked, not letting on that I didn't remember what a merle was. Everything I'd learned about Aussies' coloring had evaporated once I'd begun making the calls.

While I waited for her answer, I pulled out the pad with all my notes. Oh yes, a merle was a mottled mixture of colors, and was actually the preferred look among many Aussie buyers. This was demonstrated by the fact that breeders typically added fifty dollars or more onto an already hefty price for their merles.

"Tomorrow would be okay," she answered.

Wow, I thought, could it be this easy?

I went the following morning and drove up a dirt road onto a farm. So far, so good. I knocked on the door, which instantly set off a canine uproar. I peeked through the side window and saw two small Sheltie-like black-and-white dogs barking and scrambling at the door. I was surprised that they were so small. From the pictures and descriptions I'd seen, I thought they'd be more of a medium-sized dog—like a smallish Lab. Amid this cacophonous reception, I granted that their guarding instincts were good. I made a mental note: This would be both a plus and a minus with a young child in the house.

A middle-aged, stylishly dressed woman finally appeared and pushed the dogs back into a gated hallway before she opened the door to greet me. I asked about the size of her dogs. She explained that she was breeding miniature Aussies. She went on to extol the virtues of their diminutive size while efficiently leading me to a kennel in the back that contained the two puppies. They were very petite. The merle was quite friendly, hopping up on the gate. The black-and-white one was huddled toward the back. My heart sank. The markings were all wrong. For starters, what should have been her shawl looked more like a necktie. It wasn't Kiera. I didn't even bother to go in and try to hold her. I thanked the woman and left.

○

In a couple of days, we'd be into January and Kiera would be closing in on ten weeks old. I was feeling more and more anxious—I knew I was running out of time. I called a few more breeders the next day, all of whom were not expecting puppies until the spring. One breeder explained that the majority of puppies were usually born during the warmer months. I didn't find this statistic anomalous, just disappointing. It made sense that puppies born then would have a better chance for survival. But it wasn't doing much for my odds.

I went to bed that night beseeching Kiera to give me something more to go on. I awoke the next morning recalling no dreams. I went downstairs, got myself a cup of coffee, picked up my list, and started dialing for dogs again.

○

Breeder #6: Western Connecticut. "Yes, we have a litter that'll be ready in a week."

"Do you have any black tricolored females?" (This was what Kiera's coloring was called.)

"The females are all taken. We have three males left. You can view pictures of all of them on our Web site."

"Oh . . ." I couldn't hide the disappointment in my voice. "Thanks, but I'm looking for a female."

"You really should come and have a look anyway. This litter was sired by a champion from Gefion Hall. Every single puppy is outstanding."

"Thanks anyway," I said.

After I hung up, I did check out the pictures on the Web to see if Kiera was among her puppies. To my relief, the markings didn't match up.

○

Andrew arrived home that night a few hours after me and, wanting to be supportive, asked how my search was going.

"Any progress?" he asked, after releasing me from a hello hug.

I deflected his question. "What made you change your mind about this whole thing? I mean, this isn't a little switch."

I followed behind him as he walked over and emptied the contents of his pockets onto the hall table where he'd pick them up again on his way out in the morning. Chuckling, he replied, "You feeling a little guilty about forcing a dog on me?"

"That's exactly what I want to make sure isn't happening," I answered, now tailing him into the kitchen. "If you think I'm forcing something on you that you don't want, then this isn't a good thing, no matter how magnanimous you're trying to be."

"No, I'm okay with it," Andrew answered, "really." He rummaged though through the refrigerator looking for something to eat.

"Because you know that before these Kiera dreams started, I was perfectly happy to have a dog-free life —"

"That's just it." He turned around to face me. "You weren't happy. It's become so obvious to me that you're lost without a dog. Don't you think I see how you still look around for where she should be?"

My eyes filled up. It was true. My life felt lopsided. Not like one of my legs had been cut off so much as shortened just enough to make walking through life a noticeable chore.

"But you're committing to a long haul, and I don't want you to be sacrificing your happiness for mine."

"What you really mean is that you don't want to spend the next ten years listening to me bitching about dogs again," he said.

"That, too." I giggled and sniffled at the same time.

"Look, I can't promise that I'll always be able to stay in some Zen state with it. And I know I complained a lot about Kiera, but I really did love her. I always thought she was an amazing dog . . ." His voice cracked.

"I know you did."

"Okay." He sucked in a noisy breath. "So let's just say we both know it won't always be perfect. But if she's back . . . Well then, she needs to be back with us."

"Okay." I grinned.

"So what's the progress report?" he asked again.

I sat down at the kitchen table and scratched my head. "I feel like I'm searching for the Dalai Lama."

"What do you mean?" Andrew pulled out a chair and sat down.

"You know how, when the Dalai Lama dies, he's supposed to leave clues so the Buddhist monks can find him in his next incarnation . . ."

"Yeah, I've heard of that."

"Well, I've been given a few clues, and, with only those to go by, I'm supposed to go find Kiera. And I'm not seeing any monks lining up behind me to help with the endeavor, either. I feel like I'm running out of time."

"You'll find her." Andrew reached over and put his hand on mine. "Somehow I think this is an appointment you can't miss."

"I love you."

"I know."

○

I went back upstairs and started calling the last breeder on my list.

Breeder #7: Westchester, New York. "Yes, we have a black tri female available."

"Could you describe her markings?" I asked.

"Well, she's black with a white ruff and three white stockings. She has a little tan on the face and legs . . ."

I could hear the blood rushing through my ears. Did she say a blaze? Only three white paws? The description was close enough. I decided it would be worth the long drive to see her.

Learning as I was going, I asked if she had pictures of this puppy on her Web site. She didn't.

"When can I come and see her?" I asked, nervously holding my pen, ready to take down driving instructions.

"What, John? Excuse me a minute, my husband's yelling something at me . . ."

I could hear her speaking to her husband. He was telling her that someone had put a deposit on the puppy earlier in the day, and would be back after New Year's to pick her up.

She spoke into the receiver and started apologizing . . .

"I understand," I heard myself say. "But would you take my number down in case the buyer backs out for some reason?"

"Sure," she answered.

New Year's came and went. The phone didn't ring.

○

That was the last breeder on my list. I wouldn't let myself feel hopeless. All this meant, I told myself, was that I'd have to cast a wider net—expand the mileage radius of my search. But first I decided to go back and review my notes and comments from all the breeders, hoping to glean something; looking for some tidbit of information that could point me in the right direction.

I'd accumulated pages of material on breeder locations, litter due dates, coloration and sex of available puppies, breeding genealogy of sires and dams. As I flipped through my notes, one name started popping off the pages. Gefion Hall. Almost all of the breeders I'd contacted owned or were mating with a Gefion Hall sire or dam. But why wasn't this breeder, or place, on the Web? Could such a well-regarded breeding name with such successful lines not have a Web site? After another quick search, I was able to find a page listing Aussie breeders, where I found the address and phone number.

I called back one of the breeders who wasn't expecting a litter until late spring. I figured she'd have no reason to be offended by my asking about this Gefion Hall place.

Thankfully, the breeder was very helpful. She proceeded to give a glowing review of the dogs and breeder—and she was pretty sure that a litter was nearly ready to go. To top it off, Gefion Hall was located not much more than an hour and a half away. It was all music to my ears.

I called the place at once and got the answering machine. The woman was away and wouldn't be back until the end of the week. I left my name and number. After what felt like an eternity, the phone call came.

Yes she had a litter, but all the black tris were spoken for, except for one male. I felt as though somebody had kicked me in the stomach. I don't know why I'd decided this was the place where Kiera was, but I had. I thanked her and hung up.

I went for a walk to clear my head. I started down the road that Kiera and I had walked on together every day for the six years we'd lived in this house. We were having unusually mild weather for the first week of January. It was a beautiful, sunny, almost warm day. As I walked, I started to think that maybe these dreams really had just been some desperate wish fulfillment. Maybe I had finally gone crackers. That would make a hell of a lot more sense than thinking that my dog had reincarnated to come back to me. I knew Andrew would be secretly relieved if I let go of this madness.

That night, I went to bed physically and emotionally exhausted. Even so, a fitful night's sleep followed. I'd wake up from dreams of my old Kiera and me riding in the car together, going for hikes, playing Frisbee, snuggling, doing the things we always did together, and then I'd toss and turn for a while before dozing off again. By dawn, I was feeling completely frustrated.

I sat up, thinking that I should just forget about trying to sleep and get up to start the day. But my body was so heavy with fatigue that I decided to try one last time and flopped back down.

Somewhere between sitting and hitting the pillow, in a semiconscious state, I saw her! She was as real as if she were in the room with me. Her eyes were smiling at me and she was doing that happy vibrating thing again.

I popped back up like a jack-in-the-box and rubbed my eyes. In short order, I was wide awake. "Okay," I promised her, "I won't give up."

○

It was Saturday morning. As soon as I thought it was a respectable hour to make a phone call, I rang the breeder from the day before. I explained that I wasn't looking for a male, but would she mind if I came anyway, just to take a look at her puppies. I hadn't actually seen very many Aussies in the flesh, and I figured it'd be a good idea to get up close and personal with a few more before I decided that this was really the breed for me. She was very encouraging and agreed this was a smart idea.

I got directions and left immediately, knowing that Cait was in good hands with her dad. It didn't take as long as I'd thought, and I arrived a full twenty minutes early. I drove around to waste some time. I was in beautiful horse country with rolling hills and well-kept farms. But it wasn't long before my excitement got the better of me and I circled back. What were a few minutes between strangers?

I pulled into the long private drive that opened onto neatly maintained fenced fields. I passed by a couple of gorgeous bay foals who came loping over to see if there might be some oats in it for them. I came to a stop by the barns just past the pale yellow Colonial house.

The breeder, Georjean Hertzwig, met me at the gate with a warm handshake. She was a slender woman, I guessed somewhere in her late forties. There was nothing fussy about her; she was wearing a barn coat and jeans. As she motioned me through the first of three gates, she mentioned that she'd been expecting another party, but it was fine that I was early, and would I like to go see the puppies.

I was close on her heels as we went through the next gate to get to the field where the puppies were romping. I could see four or five pudgy little bodies bouncing off each other as we approached. They were all so full of life.

Georjean clicked the latch on the last gate that gave us entrance into the enclosure, when I saw, from across the field, a furry black-and-white blur making a dash for my legs. I scooped it up before it crashed into me.

I held her up at arm's length. There were the little tan eyebrows, and the white granny shawl, and the blaze that went clear up and over her little noggin. Not that I needed to conduct the inspection. I knew. As sure as I was standing there, I knew. I'd found her.

We were eye-to-eye, her eyes saying to mine, *What took you so long?*

CHAPTER 2

Home Again, Home Again,
Jig-Giddy-Jig

| KNEW IT was Kiera as soon as I saw her charging across the field toward me. She was doing her head-stretched out, body-barreling, I'm-comin'-to-get-ya run. It was unmistakable. I laughed out loud.

"My," Georjean chuckled, "I can't imagine what's gotten into her. She seems to really like you."

What you can't imagine, I thought, *is that this puppy of yours has been tapping her little paw for three weeks, and she's not happy that I'm late.*

Instead, I just beamed a huge smile, not willing to take my eyes off my little girl, and answered, "Yeah, I seem to have that effect on some dogs."

"That's always a good sign," Georjean commented seriously. "My dogs are pretty good judges of character. Well, would you like to see the available male puppy?"

Think fast, think fast, think fast! I screamed inside. Kiera was resting her body against my chest with both paws tucked up under my neck, and licking my chin. There was no way I could ever put her down and walk away from her now.

"Um, I know you mentioned on the phone that you had a male available, but I'm really interested in buying a female—specifically this female." (Actually, I hadn't come prepared to buy a male or female, and just hoped I had enough money in my checking account.) "Is there any chance you'd let me have her?" I asked calmly, while secretly on the verge of hyperventilating.

By this time, the rest of the puppies had wandered over to see what the commotion was about. Georjean pointed out Kiera's male sibling. He was very handsome. And he was about as interested in me as I was in him. A spectacularly beautiful little blue merle, who was mostly white with a few black spots and blue eyes, had snuck up behind me and was trying to shimmy up my leg.

Meanwhile, Georjean, evading my initial question, started running down a list of her own. She asked about my living situation and if I had any children. We have a big fenced yard, with pond and dog door. And we have three children—two teenaged boys, one in college and one who splits his week between our house and his mom's, along with one four-year-old girl—all dog-savvy. She wanted to know how much time I spent at home. Since I could often work from home, generally most of the day. She asked about my experience with dogs. I'd once worked for a vet, and I'd had dogs since I was five. She asked if I'd had an Aussie before. I hadn't, but I'd had herding breeds. And finally, she asked what happened to my last dog. I choked up at this question, and then took several minutes to tell Georjean about life with my girl, and her fatal battle with cancer.

As I was telling Kiera's story, there was a perceptible change in Georjean's face. I suspected there was something more to it than just sympathizing with my loss. When I'd finished my tale, she began to tell me about her dog, Revolution. She pointed out a striking red tri, alert but comfortably basking in the warm sunlight, over in the next paddock. This was a champion dog who was a beloved pet, and obviously meant as much to Georjean as Kiera did to me. She'd just found out that "Rev" had cancer. I was all too familiar with that look of devastation. We both hid our sniffles as well as we could, but there wasn't a thing we could do about our red eyes. In those few minutes, we'd learned as much as we needed to know about each other: We belonged to that quirky group of people who loved their dogs beyond measure, and who would always go the distance for them.

"Look," she finally said, "the other people I'm waiting for, who were supposed to arrive before you did, are the ones who want that puppy for their son. But they haven't put a deposit on her, and they've stood me up once before . . ."

I held my breath, afraid to blink.

". . . so if you're ready to buy her right now, she's yours."

Still holding on to Kiera, I had to sit down on the ground. My legs had turned to Jell-O. Puppy bedlam broke out as little roly-poly bodies started jumping and climbing all over me.

I looked up at Georjean and said, "As soon as I can get my legs to work, I'll get my checkbook out of the car." We both laughed, and I knew she knew what she'd just done for me.

I was finally able to release my grip on Kiera, and put her down to play.

○

As I went to my car, Kiera was hopping right along beside me, looking up at me the whole way. When I opened the door, she jumped in. She was ready to go. I grabbed my pocketbook, lifted Kiera up and tucked her under my arm like a little football, and walked back. That's when I noticed that the mostly white blue merle had also followed, and was waiting at the gate. When we entered again, she started weaving in and out of my feet. I had to watch where I placed each step to avoid tripping over her.

Georjean had been watching, and when I reached her, she smiled and said, "Looks like that one has a thing for you, too."

We unceremoniously sat back down on the ground to finish conducting our business. Kiera climbed in my lap and lay down. The blue merle had her paws on my shoulder and was trying to nibble on my ear. Kiera got up and started tumbling and wrestling with her.

"She's stunning. I don't think I've ever seen such a beautiful dog. When is she going to her new home?" I asked, while rummaging through my bag to find a pen. By this time, both puppies had resumed using me as their jungle gym, with the rest of the puppies looking on or playing among themselves.

"I don't know." She hesitated. "There's a guy who's offered to take her, but he lives in an apartment . . ." Her voice trailed off.

"Not enough space for her to run?" I wondered out loud.

"Well, no, not necessarily—for this one anyway." There was another hesitation. "She's deaf."

"Oh," I quietly replied as I stroked her head, now resting on my knee. Her fur was as soft as silk.

Georjean went on to explain that this was a potential hazard with merles—especially merles crossed with merles. She was quick to add that Molly—the name this little puppy went by— had come from a merle–black tri union. She also hastened to say that Molly was the first deaf puppy she'd had in all her years as a breeder. She told me that most breeders euthanize their deaf puppies, but she didn't have the heart to do it.

My brain started cooking up a crazy idea. "Do you have a phone I could use?" I asked.

She seemed a little taken aback by my abrupt segue, but said, "Sure. Let's go up to the house. We'll do the paperwork up there. And I'll see if I can find you a pen." She'd noticed that I'd been unsuccessful at locating one in my bag.

As we started walking up the hill, I explained to Georjean that I wanted to call Andrew to see if he would consider letting me take Molly, too. She stopped and grabbed my arm.

"Oh, Karen, that would be too good to be true! If Molly could stay with one of her littermates, that would be such a help for her," she told me excitedly. "Of course, you could have her for free."

Now there's a pitch, I was thinking as we resumed walking, *a two-fer sale. Two puppies for the price of one.* I shook my head. *I'm nuts; I've gone completely nuts.*

But I'd had conversations with Andrew about how, if I ever got another dog, I'd want to get two together so they could play the way only dogs could play with each other. I'd given it a lot of thought over the years, and had concluded that, as dogs are pack animals, it had to be unnatural for them to live their entire lives without another of their kind to socialize with. I'd also come to feel that way about horses and other herd animals; it just seemed wrong to have them kept alone or isolated from each other.

While I was sure Kiera had had a great life, probably better than most dogs get to have (if for no other reason than being able to go nearly everywhere with me, including work), I'm sure it could have been improved by the company of another dog. I'd grown up with a menagerie of animals. There were always at least a couple of dogs . . . and horses . . . and cats running around. I'd seen firsthand how dogs have a different life when there are other dogs around to interact with.

Andrew had always politely listened to my rantings, and even agreed with me, intellectually. Then he'd usually conclude, "You're too worried about trying to make a perfect life for all your animals and people." That'd be the end of the conversation.

With Kiera in my arms, and Molly tagging along behind, we entered Georjean's living room. There were newspapers scattered everywhere on the bare hardwood floor. These weren't discards from a manic newspaper reader, but pee papers for puppies running free inside, busy being socialized by staff and friends. A collection of four women was at various stations around the room.

It was evident that Georjean lived for her animals. There was nothing fancy in the way of furniture. There was a big wooden dining room table, a small, overflowing work desk by a window, and a couple of couches pushed back against the walls, leaving mostly open spaces for the puppies to roam. For as many animals as she routinely had in her house, there was no telltale dog or urine smell. It was the same with her barns. Earlier, she'd asked if I'd wanted to see Kiera's and Molly's mother. I said sure, so we took a walk over. The dog was resting in one of the stalls filled with fresh straw. She was indeed a sweet-tempered and friendly black tri. The barn was cleaner than my house.

One of the staff must have run ahead to relay the news that Molly might be going to a new home. As I walked over to the phone, they all smiled at me and clasped their hands together in what I'm sure was not an entirely mock prayerlike gesture.

I turned and said, "Please don't get your hopes up. I'll give it a try, but I'm thinking snowball's chance here . . ." There was nervous laughter. All of these women obviously cared very much about these dogs, and were rooting for Molly to get her happy ending.

I wished I didn't have to have this conversation with an audience present, but there was no way around it. Andrew answered on the first ring.

"I found her!" I elatedly whispered into the phone, my back turned from the women in the room.

"You what?" he asked. "I can barely hear you."

"I found her," I repeated a little more calmly and audibly.

"Wow! No kidding," Andrew let out a little whistle. "That's amazing. I knew you could do it . . . But I thought she didn't have any females."

"Yeah, me, too. It's a long story. I'll tell you when I get home. But there's something even more amazing . . ."

My mind was working furiously, trying to figure how to spin this. I imagined Andrew thinking: *What could be more amazing than thinking you've found your reincarnated dog?*

Trying not to chicken out, or worry about the consequences I might be setting in motion, I carried on.

"There's another adorable little puppy who seems to have attached herself to me as quickly as Kiera has." Before I gave him a chance to answer, I threw in all the stuff about the benefits of having two dogs, and how it would be great for Kiera. Realizing I was beginning to babble, I ended with, "And we can have her for free."

There was only a short pause. What came out of my husband's mouth next made me wonder if he'd been possessed by a body snatcher during the night.

"Uh . . . sure. I guess. The more the merrier. As long as we're getting in, we may as well get in deep."

How little did either of us know at the time how prophetic that last statement would turn out to be.

But it didn't matter then. I stood there stunned. You could have knocked me over with a feather. And then I let out a whoop, accidentally dropping the phone. I fumbled to pick it back up amid cheers and clapping. I yelled to Andrew, "You're unbelievable! I love you. I'll see you in a few hours," and hung up the receiver.

As I drove out of the driveway and turned onto the road with my little charges safely packed away in the back of my trusty old station wagon, I passed a shiny BMW with a man, woman, and boy, driving in.

I peeled out of the driveway and sped down the hill, hollering, "Kiera, we made it! We made it! We're going home!"

○

Once we were safely on the highway pointing north, and my heart rate had returned to normal, I started to think about what I'd just done. I looked up in the rearview mirror and saw two little puppy heads peeking over the backseat staring at me. My heart melted all over again.

While I'd had two dogs before, I'd never attempted to start off with two puppies at the same time. That spearmint gum jingle ran through my head, but instead of singing "double the fun," out came "double the trouble." Double the house training accidents, double the teething, double the exercising, double the obedience training . . . double, double, toil, and trouble . . . What else could I do but get silly? I was the happiest I'd been since my father died a few years before.

○

My father's death had dealt a crushing blow from which I wasn't sure I'd ever recover. He'd been my best friend, mentor, and spiritual guide through so many critical junctures in my life. I was a little afraid at the prospect of facing the next big bump, whatever that might be, without him. After all, he was the reason I'd gotten Kiera in the first place.

At a time in my life when I was single, living alone, and dogless, I saw an ad for free Sheltie puppies not very far from my parents' house and one of my offices, though I lived a few hours away. So I called up my dad and asked if he'd come look at them with me the next time I was in town, since he'd always played a major role in picking out the perfect companion for me. At the very least, I wanted him along for good luck.

Both my mother and father made the drive with me. We were escorted out back to where the puppies were. My dad watched the puppies for no more than a minute, looked over to me, and shook his head no. I reluctantly told the woman, no thanks. The visit took all of three minutes.

When we were back in the car, I asked my father why he didn't like the dogs, because it was abundantly apparent that he didn't.

He answered, "They're not mentally all there. You can do a lot better than that."

"But they were free," I said, even though I'd also thought there was something a little off with the puppies.

The "free" part was a big consideration for me, because I really didn't have the money to spend on a dog of any kind. I'd had a total of three Shelties over the years—two of which my father had given me—and I loved everything about the breed. I loved how they were inclined to bond so deeply with one person; how they were just the right size to be protective without being overbearing; and how they were so easy to train and take everywhere. (All qualities I would come to love in Aussies, though the protective quotient got bumped up a bit.) And, plain and simple, I just sorely missed the laughter and companionship they brought to my life. Now I had the space in my heart for another one.

"A free problem is still a problem," was all my father had to say.

"This isn't a good time for you to get a dog with all the traveling you do," my mother added. "It would tie you down."

"There's never a good time to get a dog, really," I said. "There's always going to be something about my life that won't be perfect. I just want one, and I'm willing to take on that responsibility and make it work."

I tightened my grip on the steering wheel and stared ahead. Against my will, tears leaked out from the corners of my eyes. My mother, just as significant and wonderful in my life as my father, noticed and asked what the matter was.

"I'm just really lonely"—my voice quavered—"and I want something else alive with me in my house besides plants."

Well, that was all that my father needed to hear.

"I'll find you a dog," he said. "We'll go look tomorrow."

"No, that's okay, Dad. Mom's right; it's probably better for me not to have a dog with all the traveling I have to do right now."

What I was really thinking was that I just couldn't afford to spend several hundred dollars.

"That's nonsense. Mom and I'll keep it when you have to be away." In my father's mind, at least, it was settled.

He called me up from his office the next morning and told me to meet him at the mall for lunch. As this was something we often did, I didn't think anything of it.

After we'd eaten, he said, "Come with me. I want to show you something."

We strolled past a few stores when I spied where he was heading.

"Dad, I don't want a dog from a pet store. I don't want to support the puppy mills that supply these kinds of stores."

"Yeah, yeah, I know. And you know under normal circumstances I wouldn't, either. We'll never do it again." He gave me an earnest look. "I promise."

"I can wait, Dad. Really, I don't want to get one from a—"

My father took my elbow and ushered me to a cage along the side wall. "There's your girl."

She was the sweetest thing I'd ever seen. It was love at first sight.

And then I noticed the red tag.

"Dad, there's a SOLD sign on her."

"Go look at whose name is on the tag."

"Oh, Dad," I whispered, and I flung my arms around him.

I later found out that my father had been busy all that morning calling breeders and striking out. Then he remembered this store, called, and discovered they did have a Sheltie. He drove over to inspect her, taking her out of her cage so he could look her over and play with her. When he decided she was the one, he wrote out a check and waited for lunch.

Kiera had proved the perfect match. We were cut from the same cloth; we both came into this life as loners, cautious of strangers, and with the instinctive drive to protect and keep safe our loved ones set on high. We'd watched each other's backs and covered each other's butts whenever it was needed. She had proved on more than one occasion that if ever I were in trouble, she would risk life and limb for me. With her by my side, I'd felt as though I could face down anything.

○

I looked up in the mirror in time to watch Kiera tumble over the backseat and climb up over the center console. She was a dog on a mission: She wanted to get onto my lap. Mission accomplished, she drifted into a sweet slumber. As I lazily scratched her velvety ears, I wondered what it was that had driven her to return to me again. I'd had no doubt that she'd made a conscious decision to come back to me. But why? We'd forged a powerful bond together, I knew. Was this reason enough for her return? Was it as simple as that: She'd found the right one for her, and that was worth coming back for? Or did she know something I didn't? Did she think her job of watching over me wasn't finished; that I was going to be in need of the kind of love only she could provide? Only time would tell.

The miles ticked past. I'd had a long drive home with Kiera that first time, too.

○

I came down the hill and around the bend, spying our 1830s farmhouse, which sat at the front of a large field. I pulled into our driveway, tooting the horn. I knew Andrew and Cait (well, at least Cait) would be anxiously waiting. With eyes shining and hair flying, Cait rounded the corner of the house at a full gallop. She let out a screech when she saw not one, but two puppies. Andrew, not quite as jubilant, walked over to help me carry the puppies to the backyard where they could run around and relieve themselves. I went in to get them some fresh water, which they quickly gulped, sending me back into the house for more.

As we watched the puppies tumble over each other, I asked Cait about names. I explained that Molly had already been given a name, and we all agreed it was a good fit for her, so she was going to stay Molly.

By this time Molly had flopped down over by Andrew. Not able to hear our voices, she'd fallen into a sound sleep. Kiera had trotted over to where we were sitting and was busy making the rounds for chin scratchings.

Referring to Kiera, I asked Andrew and Cait how they liked the name Brooke. I'd been thinking about names for the past hour while driving, thinking that maybe a new name was in order for her new life.

"Mommy, don't you know? This is Kiera. She's come back."

A shiver shot down my spine. Andrew and I looked at each other. Next, I expected to hear Rod Serling's voice from *The Twilight Zone* cutting in.

I'd never shared any of my Kiera dreams with Cait, and took great pains to make sure she didn't overhear any of the conversations I'd had with Andrew about my search for her. Any talking on the subject took place long after Cait had gone to sleep, or when she was at a friend's house. As a matter of fact, I hadn't told anyone except Andrew about this. All Cait knew was that, at some point, we'd be getting another dog. I'd been very careful about this. I hadn't wanted to set her up for disappointment if it didn't work out. And I could just hear her running into her preschool and telling the teachers that her mother was looking for her reincarnated dog. I could semi-seriously imagine the teachers discussing whether they should report me to social services for filling my child's head with such outlandish nonsense.

"What do you mean?" I asked dumbly. "I think Brooke is a nice name."

Cait walked a few paces away and called softly, "Kiera."

Kiera looked and then trotted over.

I tried to call her back. "Brooke."

Kiera didn't even turn her head. Cait gave me an exasperated look and repeated herself.

"Mommy, I'm telling you, this is Kiera."

Hearing her name, Kiera looked up at Cait.

"See." Cait pointed for emphasis. "Now you call her by her right name, and she'll come."

I looked at Andrew and asked, "Where does this kid get this stuff?"

He smiled and shrugged. "Guess she comes by it naturally."

Then I did as I was ordered. "Kiera," I called softly.

She popped around and came trotting over. All I could do was shake my head and laugh. Just to be sure this wasn't a coincidence, or Kiera just responding to whoever was speaking, we tried a few more names. The only name she answered to was Kiera.

So, Kiera it was.

My Kiera was finally home.

PART 2
Molly

CHAPTER 3

The Sound of Silence

ONE OF THE first things an observant person might notice about a bilaterally deaf dog is that its ears never move. There is no slight rise and tilt forward to show it's capturing your words. There is no cocking back to catch a random sound. No quick flicker or standing at attention to locate a sudden noise. Its ears are forever still, unused in its repertoire of expressions. This is not a deterrent to loving it, because you'll quickly get used to looking elsewhere in this dog's otherwise extensive capacity for connecting. It's all just to let you know that you've entered a world where, instead of sound, it's movement, vibration, and light that have become the means of communication. Welcome to Molly's world.

Molly was congenitally, bilaterally deaf, which meant that she was born deaf in both ears. Some might have considered her unlucky to be so stricken, because she wasn't a homozygous or double merle (of two merle parents.) But I'd discover that she was indeed very lucky, as luck would go, for she had no other physical complications.

Some deaf dogs also have associated eye problems, up to and including blindness, because the cells that grow into eyes originate in the same place where color starts, which provides the essential pigment to the ears for hearing. Because Molly only had one merle gene (heterozygous)—which resulted in her physically looking just like a double merle in patterning (she definitely had the excessive white in her coat)—she'd dodged a bullet with the eye defects.

Her deafness was caused by this lack of pigment in her inner ear, which, in turn, had caused the nerve cells of the cochlea to die off in the first few weeks of her life. Looking at any visible part of the dog's ears, inside or out, won't reveal this. Even though many white-eared dogs will be deaf, deaf dogs can also have colored ears. This was the case with Molly; she had black on both of her ears.

I also discovered that Aussies weren't the only breed affected by this merle deafness. (I would be remiss if I didn't mention here that not all double or single merles with excessive white are deaf.) Shetland Sheep Dogs, Dachshunds, Great Danes, Border Collies—actually any breed with merle patterning, and thus the merle gene—could experience deafness. (Merle is a dappled pattern, not a color.) Scrupulous breeders are careful not to breed merle to merle for exactly this reason.

I had the option of taking Molly for a BAER test, which was the only conclusive way to determine if she was deaf. BAER, short for brainstem auditory evoked response, is a hearing assessment that uses computers to read the brain's electrical activity as it responds to sound. Because the test is only calibrated to detect hearing within the normal human range, it's possible for some dogs to test deaf while still retaining some hearing in the very low or high registers. This painless procedure can be done anytime once a dog is six weeks old. Because puppy ear canals don't open until they're about two weeks old, and because it can take a couple more weeks for all the wiring to come online, so to speak, you might get an inaccurate reading having the test done any earlier.

Since BAER testing was fairly expensive, and wasn't available at many facilities (there were only three in all of New York

State, and none less than three hours away), I decided against it. I'd had Molly long enough to observe that there were no circumstances under which she responded to sound, including a high-pitched whistle. There was no doubt. A test would only confirm the obvious.

I was already quite familiar with the BAER test, as it was the same test used to check the hearing of human infants. I'd had an opportunity to learn all about this test four years earlier. When Caitlin was two weeks old, we thought she might be deaf.

At first, I thought I was lucky to have such an imperturbable baby, but after the first week, my anxiety began to build. The boys could run through the house with Kiera-1 barking full-tilt after them, with the stereo turned up loud, and the phone ringing off the hook, and she wouldn't so much as turn her head to see what all the commotion was about.

I wanted to believe it was just because Cait was an easy-going baby. I wanted to believe it was because these were all sounds that she'd become used to while she was growing inside my body. I wanted to believe anything except that she might be deaf. But Andrew and I finally had to consider that there really might be something wrong.

Because our doctor was on vacation, we'd had to meet with the covering physician. He performed a few simple tests but could give us no decisive prognosis. He said we'd simply have to wait and see. We asked if there wasn't some conclusive test. He explained about the BAER test and why it couldn't be done until she was six weeks old. We were sent home to wait. It was going to be a very long month.

When I'd been pregnant, other parents had told me how much I'd love my child. But no words could have prepared me for how profoundly I'd be swallowed up by such an inexorable love. I'd waited such a long time and had changed my life so drastically to make room for Cait. But she was so wonderful, and, in the scheme of things, being deaf would be a small price to pay to have her. It wouldn't matter if she couldn't hear; at least she was normal and healthy in every other way, I reassured myself. Many other parents had to deal with a lot worse, I chided myself. But I couldn't help feeling sad, thinking that somehow it might make her life a little harder.

I remember so well that afternoon we came home from the doctor's. I drifted into the family room, hoping to take my mind off things by watching TV. There was nothing I really wanted to watch, so I just channel-surfed: cooking show, nature show, home repair show, back to nature show. An annoying commercial blared loudly. I picked up the remote and turned off the sound. I could hear Andrew clanging around in the kitchen. I could hear the furnace fan kick on with an unsettling rumble. I brought my hands to my ears and pressed them closed until no sound could enter. I continued to conduct this experiment to see if I could comprehend what it would be like not to hear. I felt as if I were an outsider, a distant observer.

I looked up at the TV again and tried to lip-read the rest of the commercial, but I could only make out a few words here and there. I kept getting distracted by the awareness of the whoosh of blood flowing through my body with each heartbeat. Mostly, the sensation felt as though I were holding my breath deep under water. It went beyond silence, as the void goes beyond darkness.

I couldn't help but wonder if this is what had drawn me to pick up some sign language some years ago. Was I preparing myself? I tried not to draw any synchronistic conclusions. Distractedly, I looked down at my hand as though it had become possessed by someone else. It was signing the alphabet smoothly, without hesitation. I shook it hard, as though that would erase what it had just written in the air. As though that would show it that it belonged to my body, and not to these fearful thoughts.

Another week passed before our pediatrician returned from vacation. We took Cait in for an additional opinion. As he examined Cait, his motions were unhurried but efficient. I turned away to scrutinize the charts of various body parts on the wall, hoping the distraction would prevent me from grinding my teeth to dust.

I heard a foggy sound in my head, and turned around to look at him. He repeated his prognosis. Cait was fine. Hearing problems were almost always accompanied by other physical problems, he said. She had no other physical problems. He explained that some babies just take their time to fully land into their little bodies.

On the ride home, I was filled with remembering how, when I saw Cait for the very first time, I felt overwhelmed with the awareness that this would be the first and last time I'd have this experience. I knew she would be my only child. I'd learned early that every little bump, every little disappointment, every little illness she'd have would fill me with an extra helping of worry. And every little accomplishment, every newfound friend, every peaceful, happy moment would fill me with an extra helping of thankfulness. That day, it was an enormous thankfulness that engulfed me. I promised God that if I ever had a chance to repay the gift of my healthy, hearing daughter, I would do so.

Molly was the chance to make good on that promise.

○

I knew when I took Molly that teaching her would present some unique challenges, though I wasn't entirely sure what to expect. I knew only that I would love her and do everything I could to give her the most normal life she could have. I was realistic enough to know that it wouldn't always be sweetness and light, at least not in the beginning. At least not until Molly and I were able to learn to communicate with each other, and to create our own familiar and comfortable rhythms together.

My first order of business was to get myself educated about deafness in dogs. Unlike many other subjects, the Web was not overflowing with deaf dog sites. What there was, however, proved invaluable. I found the Deaf Dog Education Action Fund (DDEAF) Web site, which was full of training tips and helpful information answering many questions and dispelling many of the myths surrounding deaf dogs. There were several sites contributed by people who had deaf dogs. These were good for offering inspirational stories, experience, and encouragement. And there were two slender books on deaf dogs—both self-published—which I immediately ordered.

Otherwise, it was slim pickings. I preferred to believe this was because there were relatively few deaf dogs out there, so the subject hadn't built up a head of steam. There was one other more onerous possibility: The more I read, the more I got a sense that it was almost as though deaf dogs were breeders' dirty little secret, and not to be openly talked about—except by those people who had taken these dogs into their hearts and homes. The prevailing recommendation by the "experts" was to have deaf dogs euthanized.

There were two nagging myths presented by these experts as reason enough to dispose of these dogs: Deaf dogs were aggressive; deaf dogs were exceedingly difficult, if not impossible, to train.

There were two pieces to the aggression argument. The first was that because these deaf puppies can't hear their littermates yelp if they bite too hard in play, the deaf puppy doesn't learn how to regulate its bite to have a "softer" mouth. The second is that the dog will eventually become aggressive in self-defense, from constantly being startled by unaware people who wake or touch the dog without warning. The dog will, in effect, become a nervous wreck, and ultimately snap or bite to prevent this distress from happening.

The people who were living with and loving these dogs couldn't have disagreed more, and went to great lengths to set the record straight. I read account after account of heartwarming accomplishments these people and their dogs achieved together. Some had passed the American Kennel Club's Canine Good Citizen test. Others had passed the American Temperament Testing Society's temperament test. Some were excelling in obedience and agility. These people, while quick to admit that deaf dogs weren't for everyone, felt that if you had the time and patience, it was all quite doable.

This just confirmed what I already thought: Deaf doesn't equal stupid in dogs any more than it does in people. It just means the deaf individual—dog or person—learns to rely more on other senses, and develops a nonverbal way of communicating. And, as the Australian Shepherd was a famously intelligent breed, I was confident that Molly had inherited some of that brainpower.

I was sure that I would get out of Molly what I put into her, just as I would with Kiera. It might just take a little longer and require a little bit more creativity. I wasn't worried; I knew I would be able to find an effective way to train Molly. And one thing I had learned a long time ago was that in order to have a safe dog, you had to have a trained dog. I'd seen too many dogs whom owners had left to their own devices, out of either ignorance or laziness, who wound up being biters, chewers, jumpers, and just generally obnoxious. I'd make sure my dogs would be none of these, as I had with all my previous dogs. I'd make sure both of my dogs would be a pleasure to be around. This was a long-term investment with more than my own enjoyment at stake. It was a matter of practicality: I had my four-year-old daughter's safety to consider. And between Cait's preschool and early bedtime, I knew I'd have plenty of time to train the dogs without her having to suffer any loss of my attention.

Molly didn't disappoint; she turned out to be a stellar student. In just a few days, I'd already taught her the beginnings of how to check in, come, sit, and lie down, using hand signals and food lures. I'd cobbled together my own mixture of signing, combining dog training signs, sign language, and whatever else I concocted that worked for me. The only prerequisite was that I had to be able to make every sign with one hand, and remember the sign so I'd always be consistent. For example, the sign I used for "Sit" was really the sign for "No"—index and middle finger closing down to touch thumb. The sign I used for "No" was a finger wagging back and forth.

In order to teach Molly how to check in, if she wasn't looking at me, I'd start by stamping my foot on the floor. She'd feel the vibration and look to see what caused it. She'd look at me with her piercing blue eyes, and I'd give her the thumbs-up "Good Girl" sign and throw her a piece of cheese. I didn't put a name to this until we'd done this many times and was sure she made the connection. Then, anytime I caught her looking at me on her own, I'd point to my eye for "Look at Me," and then praise and treat. It wasn't long before I was her favorite thing to look at.

Now that I had a way to get and keep her attention, I could move on to other things. "Come" was the next natural step. Now if she looked at me for a treat, instead of throwing her the cheese, I'd hold it out in one hand for her to come and get it. Again, after many repetitions, I named the behavior with the sign "Come" (scooped hand, palm up, raised up to shoulder), and she'd come trotting over for her reward.

To teach her "Sit," I'd hold a piece of cheese at her nose. Then I'd move it back over the top of her head, which would cause her to sit in order to look up at the cheese. Once she sat, she'd get the cheese, lots of pets, and a thumbs-up. After many reps, I showed her the sign for "Sit."

Teaching her "Down" was equally easy. I'd get her to sit, and then I'd move the cheese down low from her paws along the floor. She'd crouch and then naturally lie down to get at the cheese. Once again, I'd give her the cheese, lots of pets, and the thumbs-up sign. The "Down" sign was flat hand, palm down, moving downward (dog training sign). She was noticeably bright, and seemed eager to please.

Once Molly had securely made the connection that the sign meant the action, I could begin fading the food lures. Then I would introduce a new behavior and sign. I knew we had lots more repetitions to go before that could happen, but we were well on our way. And I was convinced that training Molly not only wouldn't be difficult, but would be a pleasure for both of us.

One of the side benefits was that Kiera and Caitlin wound up learning sign language, too. Andrew could always tell when all of us girls were in the middle of one of our five-minute training sessions, because the house would all of a sudden become preternaturally quiet.

While I'd planned on teaching Kiera and Cait separately, it hadn't been necessary; they both picked it up quickly just by watching. Cait liked the idea of the dogs and us having our own secret language, so she was motivated to learn more. Seeing a chance to kill two birds with one stone—Cait could begin to learn about some of the responsibilities of dog ownership; I could cut down on some of my training time—I took full advantage. Whenever Cait showed interest, I'd place her a few feet away facing me, with Kiera in front of her. Then I'd put Molly in front of me with her rear to Kiera. I'd sign a command for Molly. Then my monkey-see, monkey-do daughter would follow suit with Kiera. This little routine became Cait's favorite way to start the day.

As far as biting her littermate too hard in play—well, Molly would occasionally do that. And then Kiera would let her have it. Molly seemed to put two and two together. After several times, Kiera trained her to have a softer mouth.

As far as the second piece, myth or not, I decided to start desensitizing Molly to being woken up and touched from behind. I wasn't about to take any chances with Cait's safety. I started reading about how to train away from potential aggressive behaviors.

As I mentioned, the concern was that waking a deaf dog would cause it to startle—like sneaking up on a hearing person and shouting "Boo!" The thinking was that eventually the dog might become aggressive as a reaction to this repeated, unexpected fright. One suggestion was to wake the dog frequently while it slept and then pop a treat in its mouth as soon as it woke up, so that it would associate positive things with being startled awake. Another suggestion was to wake the dog, but gently, by letting it sniff your hand, and then gently touch its shoulder—and then pop a treat when it woke. Another recommendation was to never disturb the dog while sleeping, so as not to startle it awake, period. I opted for the slow waking and treat.

I resolved to begin practicing this while Cait was in preschool. I didn't want any competing needs. I wanted to be able to take this low and slow—just in case. During the day, Molly always slept under my spot at the kitchen table. She especially liked to use my feet as a headrest. After a good morning's play and pee break, we all came back in to rest. Within a few minutes, both dogs were conked out.

I got my trusty pieces of cheese ready and went to work. I placed my hand in front of Molly's nose and then gently stroked her side. She awoke with a start and a look flashed across her face: some combination of feeling bewildered, scared, confused, lost. She looked up at me for help, and for a split second, she saw a stranger she didn't recognize. It was as though in waking she was wrenched again from her home before she came here, and had awakened into this strange world—as though this was her dream world and her dreams were where she belonged. The moment passed and recognition returned with a whole-body wriggle. She was happy to see me. I offered her the piece of cheese, but she was more interested in climbing up on my lap and licking my face.

I repeated this several times that day, and after that first time, she'd simply open her eyes, see that it was me, and usually go back to sleep. I also practiced touching her from behind, with the same results. She'd see that it was me, and then return to whatever it was she was doing. I practiced with her for a week. I had Andrew practice with her. Then I had some friends try. Finally, I moved on to Cait. It appeared Molly was unflappable. She loved her people, and it seemed under any circumstance was happy to see them.

Even so, I informed family and friends that Molly was not to be unnecessarily woken or touched from behind. They were to get in front of Molly first, to give her a chance to see them. I also made sure that Cait learned not to put her face close to Molly's when she wanted to wake her. I did this as much for Molly's consideration as for Cait's safety.

Except for a budding jealousy at any attention I gave Kiera (Molly had promptly put dibs on me as her own, deciding that if a little bit was good, a lot was better, and all was best), she seemed to be blooming in every way. She was full of life and full of love.

No, these deaf dog myths would not apply to Molly.

It was another issue that was waiting to detonate, one that had nothing to do with being deaf.

CHAPTER 4

The Ballyhoo Begins

THE DAY AFTER I got Kiera and Molly home, an arctic front swept over the Northeast, plunging temperatures into the single digits. It stayed frigid for the rest of January. The good news was that we got in some great skating on our pond for the first time in a few years. The bad news was that I needed to spend almost as much time outside as inside, day and night, house training my two furry puffballs.

Daytime wasn't so bad, because I could keep everyone barricaded with me in the kitchen. With its many windows cascading warm light, its old-fashioned six-burner cookstove, and its comfortably worn English rocker by the woodstove, if I had to be shut away, this was the room in which to be sequestered. With this arrangement, Cait was happy to draw or paint at the kitchen table, and I could get some work done on my laptop while keeping a close eye on the puppies. If they so much as twitched, they were in arm's reach and out the door. Often, they wouldn't even make it off the snow-covered deck. Hitting the cold air seemed to cause a spontaneous shudder followed by a quick squat. Cait and I would lavish them with praise and pets, and we'd all rush back through the sliding glass door. My three girls would plop back down in front of the fire while I'd regale them with stories of a little girl's adventures with her two dogs. This would take us to the next pee break, and so the day would go.

As Murphy's Law would have it, my puppies' urge to frolic in the snow seldom occurred during the day. This was only one of the many reasons nighttime turned into a nightmare. They also needed to go out about every two to three hours. Back in my youth, when I'd worked for a veterinarian, I'd learned that one month equals one hour in puppy bladder speak. That is, a puppy can reasonably be expected to hold its pee for as many hours as it is months old. My two were almost three months old—hence they could last almost three hours at a time. That was just enough time to get thawed out and back to sleep before I'd find myself outside in subzero weather under the stars once again. I got more sleep when Cait was a newborn, which wasn't saying much.

It finally got so ridiculous that I started sleeping on the couch in the family room downstairs, with the puppies in their crates right next to me. I used my coat for a blanket, and kept my boots by my feet, so when it was ShowTime, I'd just slip my arms in, swing my feet over into my boots, unlatch the crates with a click, and we'd all be outside in a couple of steps. One of the advantages of using the crate was that since dogs are disinclined to "wet the bed" (most animals will avoid soiling where they rest, if they can), they'd rustle around looking for a way out, which would wake up the conscientious puppy caretaker, who'd rush them outside so they could do their business in the backyard, and then all would be right with the world. Until the next round.

After several days of watching me pass through groggy on the way to delirious, Andrew finally took pity and started sharing nighttime duty.

On nights when it was my watch, Molly would invariably choose postmidnight hours to race around the backyard on a maze of paths that Andrew had snowplowed for this purpose. She'd bound over Kiera like a kangaroo, turn and come skidding back, yipping (deaf dogs' vocal cords work just fine) and nipping at her to get her to join in the play. Kiera, in self-defense from insistent pestering, would be pressed into service.

With the worst of the cold snap behind us, and some of the snow melting off during the sunny days, a new nighttime activity emerged. The puppies had gotten big enough so they could charge off the paths into the snow without disappearing. Molly, especially, took great delight in this newfound freedom; she had the explorer's heart. And with ten acres of fenced fields and woods to investigate, there were infinite possibilities. It seemed she was happiest when she was heading away from me, off on her own mission. Kiera, on the other hand, preferred to stay near, or at least keep checking back to keep me in sight. My time of watchful ease was over.

On one memorable night, Kiera and I had had enough of Molly's shenanigans and were ready to go back in. Molly had other ideas, and chose to ignore my hand signals and flashlight flicking on and off telling her that it was time. And she wasn't about to let me catch her. She'd let me get close enough to reach her collar, and as soon as she'd detect a movement of my hand in her direction, she'd take off. She was having enormous fun at her doggy *you-can't-catch-me* game. I was getting enormously aggravated. I had no better luck running from her hoping to get her to chase me. I'd used that ploy once before and she was on to it. I thought that maybe if Molly saw Kiera and me go back into the house, she wouldn't like the idea of Kiera getting any extra attention, and she wouldn't want to be left behind, thus inciting her to run back to her pack. I was wrong. She stopped just long enough to watch us go in, and then started scampering toward the back of the property. I rushed Kiera inside, got some liverwurst (Molly's favorite snack), and dashed back out.

In the thirty seconds it took me to get back outside, Molly had gone farther away from the house than she'd ever been. She started trotting across a smaller shallow pond at the rear of our property, which was made by a stream that ran through it. Instinctively, I clapped my hands and yelled out to her, even though I knew she wouldn't hear. I heard a splintering crack and she was gone.

I ripped off my heavy coat and sprinted to where I saw her go under. By the time I'd reached the pond, she'd resurfaced, but couldn't get a footing to pull herself out. I crashed through the ice to reach her. I was so pumped that I didn't even feel the frigid water flood into my boots before I was in up to my thighs. I pushed hard forward, smashing the ice in front of me as I went. I tried to grab her before she slipped under again. She was making little mewling sounds and scratching at the ice, trying to get a hold. I was desperate to get to her. She disappeared for a third time. I stuck my arms down and swished around until I felt her little body. I flung her up through the water into the night air. She was limp and shivering, but breathing. I shoved her under my sweater against my skin for warmth and raced back into the house, icy water sloshing in my boots the whole way.

She licked my hands while I rubbed her vigorously with a towel by the heat of the woodstove. She seemed none the worse for wear, though the same could not be said for me. As she curled up to fall asleep in my lap, I contemplated my first harsh reality check: If Molly was going to choose to ignore me, she was not safe—even in our contained backyard—without being on a leash. At least not until I could get her recall more reliable, and fence off the ponds, which couldn't happen until the spring thaw. My already keen vigilance just got ratcheted up a few more notches.

○

Daytimes fell more easily into a natural rhythm. Cait, Kiera, Molly, and I quickly became a pack of four. I'd feed the puppies before I'd get Cait her breakfast, at which time Andrew would leave for work. Then Cait and I would fit in a five-minute training session. If I was falling behind getting the dishes done, Cait would take over for me and get the girls practicing their "Sits" and "Downs." Then we'd all pile into the car to take Cait to preschool.

It had been Cait's idea to take the puppies with us. She knew I was always looking for ways to socialize the dogs, and she thought taking them to school so her friends could get to pet them was a smashing idea. Before I could answer, she optimistically suggested the desired answer. "Just say 'Sure,' Mommy." Then she let loose one of her thousand-kilowatt smiles. What else could I do except say, "Sure. That's a great idea, honey."

On the way to school, Cait would pass the time happily singing off-key, usually to one of her father's rock-and-roll tapes. She'd inherited his love of music but not his lilting singing voice. Unfortunately, she was as tone deaf as I was. On the high notes, Kiera would scramble up onto her and try to lick her mouth, in what I suspected were pleas for her to stop. Cait would then throw her arms around both puppies and smother them with kisses. Usually, by this time we'd have arrived at school. Cait would grab her backpack and I'd grab a puppy. Each day, I'd alternate puppies, so each one could get used to young children in very controlled and short encounters, while helping the kids learn to be gentle with puppies.

Kiera and Molly liked the attention. After the first few times, each would clamor over the other trying to get out so they could be the one to get to walk with Cait to the school door. The one staying behind would quickly snuggle into one of the down quilts in the backseat. I felt safe leaving the other puppy in the locked car, as there was no worry of heat prostration. As well, they were always in my direct sight, within a short enough distance for me to dash to if anyone attempted anything untoward.

Then my pups and I would return back home for some more R&R before I'd have to head into work. I'd crate one and take the other one out for a walk/jog, so they could get some much-needed exercise and I could spend some quality time with each one alone. Aussies were bred to be able to herd cattle and sheep on the run all day long. If I didn't get in at least a couple of miles a day for each of them, I knew I'd pay for their unspent energy at night.

I learned the hard way to crate each one of my little darlings before taking the other out. The first time I took Molly, I'd gated Kiera in the kitchen with a four-foot, childproof gate. On our return, to my surprise, there was Kiera, sitting pretty as a picture by the front door in the living room. Don't ask me how she managed to scale that gate, but she did. When it was Molly's turn to be left behind, I came back to find that anything chewable in the kitchen had been chewed (except her chew toys, of course): rug, chair leg, back end of rocker. That was the end of kitchen privileges; crates for one and all.

○

During the first few weeks, I was mostly concentrating on house training.

Kiera was a quick study. She got it in three days. Then, whenever she needed to go, she'd move to the door and look over at me. If I wasn't speedy enough for her, she'd give a little yip for emphasis. Molly, on the other hand, was completely unconcerned about where she was when she was ready to relieve herself. I finally had to roll up the rugs in the kitchen and family room, and send them off to be professionally cleaned. Bare wood floors were much easier to deal with.

I knew enough not to attribute human qualities, such as spite or stubbornness, to Molly's dog behavior. Any animal behaviorist (several of whom I would get to know in the days and months ahead) would instruct that dogs just aren't calculating in the way people can be. They'd go on to say that if someone is having a problem with a dog, the problem would really be in the person's lack of understanding or misinterpretation of dog behavior.

I was also aware that Kiera got it unusually fast, and it wasn't fair to hold Molly to that standard. I wasn't expecting them to get everything at the same pace, either, but it seemed as though, even after a few weeks, Molly wasn't even starting to make the connection. This wasn't because I wasn't being consistent enough; I was getting them out immediately on waking, fifteen minutes after eating or playing, and at least every hour otherwise. Molly would relieve herself, as would Kiera. They would both be petted and praised profusely. We'd come back inside and Molly would relieve herself again shortly thereafter. So I had to look elsewhere for the cause.

Over the almost two months that I'd had Kiera and Molly (now four and a half months old), my training philosophy had been dramatically altered. Noted dog trainer Barbara Woodhouse, along with the Monks of New Skete, both traditionally based, had been my previous guiding lights on all things dog-related. But all the reading I'd done on deaf dog training introduced me to the concept of teaching with positive reinforcement. This required no traditionally based physical force or "corrections" (on occasion a polite euphemism for physical punishment), but rather embodied the idea of ignoring what the dog was doing wrong, and capturing what the dog was doing right and rewarding that—at least initially with food, as well as, of course, with lavish praise, play, and anything else the dog highly valued.

I'd never been one to strike my dogs. So I never would have considered whacking Molly or rubbing her nose in her pee, either. That seemed rather barbaric to me. And while I understood the value of gaining your dog's respect, the "alpha roll" and other displays of human physical force struck me as extreme. The worst any of my dogs ever got was a sharp voice, which was nearly always reprimand enough. If they were really being incorrigible, I might make a low growl for emphasis. Nothing more was ever required.

But, in training, I had used physical force to push them into sits, and press them into downs. And I'd always shied away from using food as rewards because I figured then I'd always be stuck with having to use food. All of my other dogs had been apt pupils, and learned well under these traditional methods, so why change? As I thought about it, if there was a way I could get my dogs to *want* to learn, instead of being forced to learn, that could only be better for the dogs, and therefore for me.

Once convinced by all the reading I was doing that it wouldn't be a problem to eventually wean the food out of the training, I thought this newfangled way was worth a shot. Within a few days, I'd become a convert. The speed at which these puppies were learning was an awesome thing to watch. You never saw two such excited creatures when they'd see me strap on my training pouch (a fanny pack that contained cut-up cheese, clasped around my waist for handy access). It was as if they were saying, *Yippee! Mom's gone for the food pouch. We're gonna get to have some fun now!* My dogs were enthusiastic about training, and I was sold.

But I still had this conundrum on my hands. As I'd said, Molly was learning everything thing else as quickly as Kiera. So why wasn't she getting the "go outside" thing?

It took me a while but I finally figured out that I was lacking two of the key ingredients for her success. I had not thought to reward Molly with food for going outside. Nor had I attached a sign to put the desired behavior on cue. I was excited by this discovery, and hopeful that I had found the solution.

Sure enough, by the end of the week, Molly had made the breakthrough—she got it! While I was thrilled to have solved the mystery, this served as a more important lesson in my understanding of training and, specifically, training with Molly. That, and I was eager for the prospect of being able to put the rugs back down on my cold floors.

○

A couple of weeks later, I decided to enroll just Kiera and me into an obedience class. Specifically, I was looking for guidance on weaning the food rewards, because I'd found the information I read on how to do this confusing. Cait, now five, immediately volunteered to come along. She liked training the dogs and especially loved being anywhere I was. And most times I really loved having Cait with me; she was great company. But this wasn't one of those times. Andrew took one look at my face and got that this was really an excuse for me to be alone with Kiera. He quickly came to my rescue and offered to take Cait and Molly for a walk while I was at class, so she wouldn't feel left out. Cait was dubious about the offer until Andrew said she could hold Molly's leash the whole time, something I rarely let her do. That clinched the deal, and I breathed a sigh of relief.

It was true that I was interested in keeping Kiera socialized, but it was more true that it would give me time alone with her, for which I was sorely feeling the need. Molly had pretty much commandeered me for herself, and did her best to keep Kiera away. I was happy to give Molly the love and attention she craved; she was very affectionate and sweet with me. But I'd also learned that if I wanted to spend time with Kiera, I had to either crate Molly in the other room or take Kiera for a walk. If I didn't, Molly would come over, give a little snarl, and insert herself between the two of us. She had succeeded at pushing Kiera into second-dog status; Kiera eventually stopped trying to come over to me. It had never occurred to me that I'd have to deal with the whole pack-pecking-order thing, but here it was.

The class I'd enrolled in was presented as positive training. I thought this would be a chance for me to learn more about this method I'd been experimenting with on my own. I was looking forward to having someone watch what I was doing to give me feedback. Even though I was getting really nice results with my pups, I felt there was so much more I needed to learn.

Kiera and I were one of the first to arrive at the Mahogany Ridge Dog Training and Daycare Center, which was set far back from the road. The complex comprised a small, sky-blue house that had been converted into an office, dog food store, and back room for the dogs that connected to a huge fenced back-yard. The training center was a converted garage. We made our way to the classroom and waited for all the others to arrive. Kiera took this opportunity to alternately snuggle in my lap and put her paws around my neck to give me puppy kisses. She seemed as relieved and happy as I was to have this time all to ourselves. It felt like old times.

My pockets were full of treats, and we were ready to go. People and dogs began trickling in. First, a very shy Boxer named Stella entered with her "mom." Then a very rambunc-tious and huge Australian Shepherd with a tail made a noisy en-trance with his "dad." Then a playful black Lab with her parents. And finally a big hairy Newfoundland brought up the rear with his mom. We were all present and accounted for.

Theresa Richmond, our teacher, an upbeat woman with a permanent twinkle in her eye, introduced herself and then asked each one of us to do the same. Turned out, both the Boxer and Newfoundland had been saved from shelters and were in for re-medial training. The Aussie had been "rescued," which, I learned, meant his previous owner had given him up to be fostered until people who were dedicated to this breed were able to find him a new home. The young man who'd taken this Aussie into his heart seemed unaffected by his somewhat wacky charge. Kiera and the Lab were the only puppies in the class, and the only dogs who'd not been rehomed.

As the class got under way, I discovered it was really an amalgam of both traditional and positive training. Food was used, with this explanation given: Who would go to work if there weren't a paycheck in it? Dogs aren't any different; they work better if they know there's a reward at the end of it.

Okay, I could get behind that thinking. I already believed in the value of encouraging with rewards, but I also began to re-think the need for balance by establishing boundaries on both sides of the "right" and "wrong" coin. This offered the benefit of giving feedback on what the dog was doing correctly and in-correctly. Thus, by setting both parameters, dogs had a much clearer understanding of what was expected of them. As long as no severe methods were used, such as jerking, hitting, or "hang-ing" dogs from the leash (which they weren't), I was going to keep an open mind.

Theresa asked if she could use Kiera to help her demonstrate the techniques. Before I could explain that I'd already been working with Kiera, she whisked her into the center of the room. What happened next turned into an Abbott and Costello routine.

Theresa began by explaining how we were to teach "Sit." She was going to hold a piece of food up over Kiera's head, getting her to look up, while gently pushing down on her rear until she sat. Looking around at the class, Theresa first demonstrated the dog training sign for "Sit" by raising her hand (palm up and flat). Kiera, who was standing a little bit behind her, sat. The class tit-tered. Theresa looked around to see what was so funny. By this time, Kiera had popped back up looking for her treat. Theresa, wanting to make sure everyone saw the first demonstration, repeated the hand movement. Kiera sat again. The class giggled. Kiera popped back up. Theresa looked around.

"All right, you guys. What's so funny? Is my zipper down; do I have spinach in my teeth?" Theresa asked, good-naturedly.

Then she turned to Kiera and said, "Are you blowing raspberries behind my back, you little rascal?"

She leaned over and raised her hands in a shrugging motion to underscore her words. Kiera sat. The class roared.

Theresa got the picture and laughed, too. "The joke's on me, I see." She looked over at me and smiled. "That definitely deserves a treat!" She tossed a liver bit and Kiera caught it. "Let's see what else this little smarty-pants knows."

She proceeded to put Kiera through her paces. Sit, down, come, stay, heel. Kiera performed right on cue—even to the heel command, which I hadn't taught her yet. Theresa obviously had impressive skills and a natural touch with dogs. Kiera got a round of appreciative applause as Theresa walked her back to me.

As she handed Kiera over, she said, "You, I want to see after class."

She then borrowed the Lab, and the class resumed without incident for the next half hour. As the rest of the class left, Theresa motioned for me to join her.

I immediately began apologizing and explaining.

Theresa interrupted. "Hey, I'm always thrilled to see a trained dog. How could I be mad at that? I'm just wondering what you're hoping to get out of this class."

I began explaining about my situation with Molly and Kiera, and how I was looking for a way to get some quality time alone with Kiera. I also explained that I was looking for a way to get more socializing in for Kiera, as well as continuing guidance on what I'd done so far.

She listened, nodded, and agreed those were good reasons. Then she offered, "Why don't you consider taking an advanced obedience class? You and Kiera would probably get more out of that."

"I would, except I don't feel that I really know what I'm doing yet with fading the food. And there are still a few basics she doesn't know yet."

"Okay, it's up to you."

I thanked her and turned to leave.

"By the way . . . ," Theresa began.

I turned back.

"Did you say that Kiera and Molly are siblings?"

"Yeah, they are," I answered. "Why?"

"Sometimes issues come up, but if you're not seeing any, that's great."

She walked me to the door, gave Kiera a pat, and said good night.

I wasn't ready to go home just yet, so I took Kiera to the park. I grabbed a dog blanket from the backseat and spread it out on the ground. Kiera and I struck a familiar pose as we lay together looking up at the stars, with her snuggled in the crook of my arm, her head rising and falling with my chest. Being with Kiera out under a night sky was something that always filled my soul with happiness.

CHAPTER 5

Beginning of the Slippery Slope

I YELLED OVER the din to Cait, who was standing on the other side of the kitchen table. "Go into the family room, and close the door behind you! Now!"

Cait was paralyzed, her little mouth gaping in horror.

"Go. Now!" I sternly ordered again. Quickly looking up, I could see she was still frozen stuck. *"Get out of here!"* I finally bellowed, worried for her safety. The dogs were flying over and around each other, and moving her way. I wasn't going to be able to get to her before they would.

I heard her make a run for it and shut the door behind her. I couldn't look because I was too busy frantically trying to break up the fight. I'd already made the mistake of sticking my hand down to try to separate them, and got a nice puncture wound for my efforts.

The fur was, quite literally, flying. Ripped tufts were eddying around them. The air was filled with fierce snarls, growls, and biting sounds. They were a whirling blur at each other's throats and heads, body-slamming and punching each other with their front legs while standing on their hind legs. I'd never heard or seen anything like it.

Looking for a way to break them apart, I scanned for something handy to throw at them. I grabbed a couple of small plastic bowls that were sitting on the counter and hurled them. The bowls bounced off and skittered across the floor, having no effect. I ripped the roll of paper towels out of the holder and tried to wedge that between them. They were moving so fast, and were so intent on getting at each other, that I couldn't hold on to the towels for long before they, too, went rolling away on the floor.

In a last-ditch effort, I ran around behind Kiera and gripped her rear. In one swift motion, I pulled her back and spun her around, jerking her up and over my head. Breathing hard, I held her up there in a suspended state, waiting for whatever was going to happen next.

As suddenly as it broke out, it was quiet. It was over in less than two minutes, though it had felt considerably longer. Molly didn't rush me to try to get at Kiera. Kiera didn't try to struggle free from my hands to get at Molly. It was over. For now at least.

Cait whimpered from the other side of the door, "Mama, Mama are you all right? Mama?"

"Yes, honey, I'm fine and the dogs are fine. Don't come in yet. Let me get them into their crates first."

"Okay, Mama." I heard her slump down against the back side of the door.

I checked Kiera over first. She licked my face while I examined her head. There was no broken skin. I stuffed her in her crate. Molly had gone over to her spot under the table and lay down as if nothing had happened. I inspected her, and she, too, was fine. I locked her into her crate. Then I went and scooped Cait up into my arms and we sat on the couch. She snuggled into me and then noticed the oozing wound on my hand.

"Oh, Mommy! Look what happened!" She pulled my hand over to get a better look.

"It's nothing, honey. It was an accident. It was my fault for sticking my hand where it didn't belong."

It really was nothing. Fortunately, they still had puppy teeth, which didn't have the power to do much damage—though the force of the bite was enough to make my hand ache.

Cait got up and warily went into the kitchen, moving with her back toward the wall and keeping her eyes on the dogs. They both lay quietly in their crates, looking at her. I asked her what she was doing.

"I'm getting you a Band-Aid to fix your booboo," she answered, returning with one in hand. She'd brought a disinfectant wipe, too, remembering this was how I treated her "booboos."

Cait was a natural healer. She had an instinct for knowing what to do to make somebody feel better. Since birth, she seemed filled with an inordinate amount of compassion and empathy. She busied herself with cleaning off the wound and bandaging it up.

"There," she said, admiring her work, "good as new," repeating what I always said to her.

We stayed cuddled on the couch for a while in an effort to calm down and reassure ourselves everything was all right. We'd had quite a fright.

"Mommy, I thought they loved each other. What made them fight?" Cait asked, looking up at me wide-eyed.

"I'm not sure, sweetie, I didn't see what started it. Did you see what they were doing before it all started?"

Anxious to relay what she'd seen, Cait hopped up on her knees and started talking excitedly with her hands flying around like a cop directing traffic. "Kiera just wanted to lay down in Molly's spot under the table by your chair." She pointed to an invisible chair. "I don't know why Molly cared because she was laying in Kiera's spot under McLean's chair." She pointed in the opposite direction. "Anyway, Molly went over and growled and snapped at her. I think she might have gotten the end of Kiera's nose. Then the next thing they were fighting." Cait sank back down into the couch, her voice dwindling to a whisper as she finished telling her tale.

I was no expert on animal behavior, but it seemed, from what Cait described, that there was a bid going on for who was going to be the alpha dog to rule not only me, but also prime real estate. Having had the dogs for two months now, I reflected back on how I'd been noticing for the last few weeks that Molly wanted me exclusively for herself. She wouldn't allow Kiera to come close, and would insert herself between the two of us to prevent this. Kiera seemed to have accepted this display of dominance and usually stayed a respectful distance, lying down at one of her spots across the room. If I wanted to have contact with Kiera, I'd have to go over to her.

I wasn't quite sure what to make of this new wrinkle. I'd seen dogs have skirmishes over dominance issues before. But not as intense as this. And never my own dogs.

The next morning, once Cait was safely at preschool, I decided to call Theresa to find out more about her comment that "issues sometimes come up." Thankfully, she was available to talk with me. She detailed her background, explaining that she had a lot of training and experience in handling dog aggression. And while she'd been hoping she wouldn't get a call from me, she wasn't surprised that she had.

Obviously, she knew something I didn't. I asked her what she meant. She explained that it wasn't unusual for same-sex siblings to eventually have difficulty getting along, unless one of the dogs was significantly more submissive than the other. She was a little concerned that my dogs seemed too evenly matched on the dominance scale, and added that this could turn into a real problem. She asked for more details so she could better understand what was going on.

I described Kiera and Molly's behavioral history together, which, up until then, had been mostly affectionate and playful.

Then I added what I knew about this latest circumstance. She asked several more questions about their breeding, sleeping arrangements, food, toys, exercise, and so on, then concurred with my assessment. At this point, she didn't think one incident warranted keeping them permanently apart. She recommended I just let them work it out. She reassured me that it almost always sounded and looked worse than it was, and that most of it was probably just a display. She also warned that this might sporadically continue until Molly was successful at asserting her dominance. As Theresa continued talking, I made a mental note to keep a hefty mop handy; if things really got out of hand, I could use the mop to help separate them without hurting them or getting hurt myself.

I asked her if, while Molly and Kiera were working this out, she felt this would pose any danger to Cait. She said that from what I told her, this behavior was not triggered by, nor had anything to do with Cait, so she thought it very unlikely that Cait would be harmed unless she tried to get in the middle of it. I thanked her and hung up.

I went over and sat between the two crates so I could scratch both puppies' heads. "Okay, here's the deal," I said, "I'm going to try letting you two back out again. If there's so much as a curled lip, you're both going back into lockup. Got it?" (I knew Theresa had said to just let them work it out, but I wasn't up for another blowout in the same day. This was going to take some getting used to.)

I looked at each of them; they appeared to listen intently. Well, at least Kiera listened. I knew Molly could tell by my face and signing that I meant business. I let them out. Kiera went to the door to let me know she needed to go out. I made the "Bathroom" sign for Molly to follow. They went outside and had a perfectly civilized romp, making what had happened earlier seem like a bad dream. When we came in, they both went to their respective spots and slept until it was time for me to pick up Cait.

A few days passed without incident. I was feeling drained from being on constant alert, looking for any signs indicating another rumble. I instructed Cait not to get on the floor with her face near the puppies. It was an unnecessary directive. On her own, Cait had withdrawn most of her affection toward Kiera and Molly. She preferred to give them a wide berth; her trust had been shaken. I figured I could help her mend that once I was sure things were back in order with the dogs. Until then, I was just as glad to have her keep her distance.

In the meantime, realizing that I had entered into territory about which I was clueless, I bought every book I could find on dog behavior. And what a mixed bag it was. Theories ranged from dogs having no emotions and only conditioned reflex behavior, to dogs having emotions nearly as rich and complex as humans. Methods of handling aggression varied from unerringly and forcefully showing the dog who's boss, to learning to read the cues leading up to the aggressive behavior and interceding with redirected behavior, thereby preventing a full-blown outburst.

How was anybody supposed to sift through all of these conflicting views, never mind make sense out of it, or apply any of it? I started by tossing out the books that advocated what I considered extreme measures.

○

I loved Molly as much as I did Kiera, although in a different way. I loved snuggling with her and running my fingers through her exquisite silken fur. I loved her playfulness and spirit. I loved how she always knew what she wanted and made no bones about it. It was a quality that I could stand some strengthening in myself. Life for her was straightforward and simple: You go after what you want until you get it, devil be damned.

But it made me sad that Kiera had become reluctant to come over to me and, overall, avoided me when Molly was nearby, which was pretty much all the time. In an odd way, it felt as though I had lost Kiera for a second time. I wished that I wasn't being put into a position where I had to choose one dog over the other in order to keep the peace.

But I had enough sense to let this be. I understood that this was part of them working out an arrangement that both dogs could live with. And I wanted them to get it worked out fast, because I wasn't willing to live with two dogs that I'd have to worry about keeping separated.

And it seemed in some way that Kiera understood all of this even better than I. It was as if, when she looked at me from across the room, she was saying, *No worries. We have all the time in the world. No point in sweating the small stuff.* As though she knew her time would come again, and she'd just watch and wait until then.

A few days later, I was sitting in the rocker reading *The Culture Clash* by Jean Donaldson, a book I found to be an incredibly valuable and illuminating exposition on dog behavior and aggression. Molly was lying on my feet and Kiera was resting under her spot at the table. Out of the corner of my eye, I saw Kiera get up and start to walk past Molly to get to the door — something she'd done a hundred times before. Molly's eyes turned steely blue and she stiffened, her hair raising slightly. My blood ran cold. I could see it happening in slow motion and couldn't get any of my body parts to move. Kiera slowed, circled out wider, and kept walking. Molly gave a warning growl and then lunged. They were on each other in one bound. I was watching an instant replay of the first encounter. They were frothing and frenzied, caught in a violent embrace.

"Stop it! Stop it!" I screamed. Finally able to unlock my legs, I jumped up and stomped my foot so Molly could feel the vibration through the floor. I signed and yelled, *"Knock it off!"*

Kiera might as well as have been deaf, too. Neither dog took her eyes off the other. Then Molly succeeded in bowling Kiera over and was at her throat.

That was the tipping point.

Kiera went ballistic. She extricated herself and flung herself at Molly with a vengeful force. The fighting reached a feverish pitch. I ran to get the mop and tried to shove it between the two. They were close enough to the door so that I was able to open the slider and push Molly out, since she was the closest one to it. I quickly slammed the door shut and leaned over, feeling sick to my stomach. They were still snarling, spitting, and scratching at each other through the glass. I reached over and grabbed Kiera. There was some blood on her head. I combed through her fur to see if there was a hole or tear. There wasn't, though I did find one of Molly's baby teeth sticking out of her head. The blood had come from Molly's bleeding gums. I shoved Kiera in her crate, checked Molly, and went to the phone.

Theresa's first question was whether either dog had been injured. I had to admit that they hadn't. She reiterated her earlier advice: Even though it sounded and looked awful, she encouraged me to let them keep at it until one of them emerged as the accepted alpha. I thanked her again and hung up. By now, I'd read enough behavior books to know that this was the conventional wisdom, but the thought of living with this until they worked it out was excruciating. I was relieved that Cait had been at school.

As awful as I felt, I really did want to get past this. There was only one thing to do; I sucked in a deep breath and forced myself to open the crates once more. I felt like I needed to throw up. I really wasn't sure I had the stomach for this. Molly immediately came out of her crate to be near me again. Kiera just looked at me and remained at the back of her crate with the door open. I tried to coax her out, but she just laid her head down on her paws and averted her eyes. It was as though she was afraid to even risk looking at me.

About ten minutes later, Kiera got up to come out of her crate. As soon as she cleared the door, Molly went at her and they were tangled up again. I made myself go into the other room and closed the door to prevent myself from breaking them apart. I paced like a caged animal.

Two minutes went by.

Three minutes.

Five minutes.

Instead of the noises abating, they were getting worse. I'd taken all I could stand. That was it. I blasted back into the kitchen like a hurricane, yelling at the top of my lungs. I was so flipped out and angry that, before I could think about what I was doing, I grabbed each of them by the scruff and threw them apart. They tried to get back at each other and I swung my foot at whoever came near. They backed away from me as I stood there like the Karate Kid, feet apart, crouched, arms out, and ready to chop or kick at the first thing that came near. They both looked at me as if I were crazy. No doubt, at that moment, I was. As far as I was concerned, this was war now and I'd do whatever I had to in order to keep them apart. They got the message and stopped.

Once again, I inspected them. After finding no injuries, I decided not to crate them. I wanted to take advantage of the anger I was feeling, because it gave me the courage and the detachment I needed to just wait and see what would happen next.

If they were living in the wild, there wouldn't be some well-meaning softy getting in the middle of their fights. They'd be left alone to go at it until there was an undisputed winner. I had to stop looking at my dogs as my babies that I felt compelled to protect from each other, and start seeing them as the sometimes wild things they were, with instincts and rules that weren't always going to fit within my sensibilities. I had to accept that I wasn't going to be able to overrule those instincts either. There was unfinished business. I knew I could muscle them to behave, and they might even appear to get along. But then I'd always have to worry about what would happen if I wasn't there to enforce the peace. I came to think that Theresa was right: There wasn't going to be any way around it. They had to work it out.

I didn't have to wait long. Within the hour, another battle was waged. As hard as I tried to let it run its course, I couldn't. After several minutes, again I interceded. This time I did put them in their crates. Three times in one day was enough. Even though I worried that I was ultimately making matters worse by not letting them continue through until it was all finished, I couldn't take any more. My nerves were fried.

I was starting to feel that I was in over my head. I called Theresa again and asked her if she would come over to evaluate the situation firsthand. She agreed to come out the next morning.

It was time for me to pick up Cait from school. I'd decided that I would always have one dog crated at all times when Cait was around. I didn't want her to witness any more scenes. I knew I could let the dogs free once Andrew was home from work. By that time in the evening, the dogs were pretty tired out, and somehow Andrew's presence seemed to change the mix. I'd observed that Molly lost interest in marshaling Kiera around once Andrew arrived, and there'd never been a hint of trouble.

○

I was outside playing with Molly when Theresa pulled up. Even though Molly had never met Theresa before, she greeted her with licks and wags. Theresa got right to work. She asked if I'd bring Kiera out so she could watch what happened. I reminded her that Molly was deaf, and I wouldn't be able to let her off-leash outside, so we went into the kitchen. Kiera, who was resting by the stove, looked up but didn't come over, even though she'd become quite friendly with Theresa through the obedience class.

We sat and talked, and just let the dogs be. I pelted Theresa with questions. As she answered, she kept her eyes on the dogs. Molly had come over for pets. Theresa called Kiera over, too. She obediently came. She put Molly and Kiera into a side-by-side sit, and then unobtrusively hooked a finger around each collar. She didn't pet, talk to, or even look at them. She just sat with a finger looped around each one's collar, waiting.

I asked her what she was doing. She said she was looking to see something and when she was finished, she'd be glad to explain. Molly was perfectly content to just sit there. After a minute, Kiera started fidgeting, and strained to pull away. Theresa let them both go. Kiera went back to her spot and just stood. Molly lay down by Theresa.

"There's your dominant dog," she said, pointing to Kiera.

"But Molly's always the one who starts the fights," I answered, bewildered by her pronouncement.

"Molly is close enough in dominance to want to try to overthrow Kiera. She's making her bid for top dog."

Theresa stayed and talked for a while longer. She explained, "Long, drawn-out threat displays like Kiera and Molly are doing are what middle-ranking dogs do when they're not sure of their social position."

"But what about the danger of them going at it for several minutes?" I asked.

She reassured me, "It's not uncommon for dogs to bluff and threaten each other for that long, or even longer. If it does break out into a full-blown fight, the fight can also seem to go on forever and be extremely noisy, as you've seen for yourself. It can sound and look like the dogs are trying to kill each other."

I nodded in agreement, having witnessed this exact dynamic. It did look as though they wanted to kill each other.

Theresa cautioned, "So far, you've been lucky."

"How so?" I asked, not really wanting to hear that it could get worse.

"It's the short, silent fights you need to be concerned about."

Oh great, I thought, *one more thing to worry about.*

She wrapped up the conversation by restating, "When fights go on and on, and the dogs continue to growl and snarl, it's because they're still feeling each other out. This means the bites are usually inhibited. Each dog is still trying to bluff the other, and neither has really committed herself to an all-out attack. These fights are more of a psychological battle than a physical one."

"Okay," I joked, "I'll keep telling myself that when it sounds like the end of the world has come."

"You can handle this. You're doing fine." She smiled.

I nodded, but I didn't feel that I was doing fine at all. I didn't want her to leave me alone with my dogs. I really wanted her to take them with her until they got it all worked out. I didn't know how I was going to acquire the nerves of steel I'd need to get through this.

There was another question I wanted to ask, but didn't: What happened if they didn't get this worked out? I didn't ask because I wasn't ready to contemplate anything other than a positive outcome. Besides, if it didn't work out, I knew what the answer would be.

She got up to leave. "Look at it this way: By the time you're done learning about all this dog behavior, you'll be ready for a second career as a dog trainer."

"Thanks, but I think I'll keep my day job." We both laughed.

Of course, there had been no outbreak while she was there. Her parting recommendation was that, because the hierarchy was unstable and Molly was the one making the serious effort to be the dominant dog, I try to support Molly's efforts in rising to the top by feeding her first, letting her go through doors first, giving her all the attention, and on and on. I'd been doing that, but I agreed to continue.

◯

While the dogs were so central to my daily life, they were only peripherally so to Andrew's. Nearly all dog activities and "incidents" took place while Andrew was at work. His primary experiences with them were at night when they were tired and sleepy—and as the saying goes, a tired dog is a good dog. It was time for me to let him in on what was going on.

That night, I decided to talk to Andrew about the fighting. I'd been reluctant to tell him, partially, I think, because I was trying to stay in denial, telling myself this would all get resolved after a few skirmishes. And, after having told him the reason I wanted to get Molly was so that Kiera would have a playmate to make her life even better, I was feeling embarrassed by what I now considered my naïveté. And I was feeling depressed that it seemed the opposite was happening. Kiera and Molly played together less and less, and their encounters seemed to be getting fiercer. I was beginning to think that all I'd done was create a huge mess that I didn't know how to solve.

But there was no one better than Andrew at helping me think out loud and sort out my feelings, both of which I desperately needed to do. He also had a right to know that something was going on that could affect Cait's safety and my sanity.

After Cait had gone to bed, I went into the family room where Andrew was watching TV. He looked over at me and asked, "What's up?"

I went over, sat down next to him on the couch, and tucked myself under his arm. Then I unloaded everything that had been happening, concluding with Theresa's assessment of the situation.

Andrew would have been well within his rights to use this as a chance to rub in an *I told you so*, or to point out the *Kiera-will-have-a-friend* debacle. He didn't. He just listened, raised an eyebrow, and asked, "So what do you make of Theresa's analysis?"

"That's the thing," I began. "I saw the same thing, but had a totally different reaction to what was happening."

"What did you see?"

"I saw Kiera afraid to greet Theresa with Molly so near. And I saw Kiera feeling uncomfortable and defensive at being held so close to Molly. When Theresa let them go, Kiera couldn't get away from Molly and over to her spot fast enough."

"Did you ask Theresa about that as a possible explanation of what was going on?" Andrew shifted his weight and massaged his brow as the seriousness of the situation began to sink in.

"No, I was really just focused on what she was saying. And I'm not sure she'd think that mattered. Her point is that Kiera and Molly are so closely matched in dominance, neither one wants to let the other be the boss."

"So what does that mean?"

I was so tired and worn out by the whole thing that my eyes welled up. "So far, what it means is that it ain't over till it's over. The fighting is going to continue until one of them concedes."

Andrew thought for a moment and then asked, "If it's common knowledge among dog people that same-sex siblings are likely to have a problem, shouldn't Georjean have known this as a breeder?"

I'd had that same thought awhile back and dismissed it. I answered, "I don't think there were any signs pointing to problems at the time I got the puppies from Georjean. If you remember, they got along fine and played great together for the first month we had them." I explained further, "It's not like all littermates or same-sex dogs have problems. It's only when dogs are too evenly matched in dominance that it becomes a problem.

Dogs need a clear hierarchy; Kiera and Molly haven't been able to establish one. That's the problem."

Andrew nodded and then looked over at the dogs. They had plopped themselves in front of us and were sound asleep. Molly was on my feet, and Kiera was across the room.

"I can also start running with each of them," he offered. "What are they—almost six months old now? Old enough to go a mile or two, aren't they? That might tire them out more, so there's less energy to fight."

It was moments like these that reminded me why I loved my husband so much.

"I'm not sure," I answered. "I don't think you're supposed to run distances with them until their bones finish growing. Maybe a mile would be okay. I'll find out."

After ten years of marriage, Andrew never ceased to amaze me. He'd have every right to wash his hands of the whole thing. After all, he'd been very vocal about his preference not to have any more dogs. But there was a larger part of Andrew's makeup at work. I knew I could always count on him when the chips were down. And the chips were definitely down.

◯

It'd been a few days since Theresa's visit. I was trying to support Molly as alpha dog, as she had suggested. And I got every book on Aussies, training, and dog aggression I could find. I was beginning to build quite a library. There had been a couple of scuffles, though nothing terribly awful. And these encounters had ended on their own, so I felt encouraged that maybe some progress was being made.

One of the books I found fascinating was Turid Rugaas's book on calming signals. She was a Norwegian woman who had dedicated years to deciphering the ways in which dogs used body language to communicate both aggression and submission.

For instance, according to Rugaas, lip licking and yawning were ways dogs let other dogs know they were nonthreatening. And, alternatively, a stiff raised tail, staring, and pointing off another dog (standing rigidly in line, nose-to-nose) indicated an attempt at dominance and possibly aggression if the other dog didn't offer a calming signal to defuse the situation.

I found it helpful to see if I could pick out any of the behaviors that led up to a fight breaking out. What I began observing was that Molly could usually, very effectively, control Kiera by staring and curling her lip. Kiera would respond by averting her eyes, slowing her movements, or moving farther away. I hoped that by trying to turn myself into a behavioral scientist, I'd be able to contain my urge to separate them, which was always my first inclination.

I began taking each dog into town more frequently for walks. It gave me a chance to really focus my attention on whoever was with me. It also gave me the chance to observe each one around human and animal strangers. I was hoping that this exercise would help me get better at catching and identifying their aggressing and calming signals, and therefore help me understand what was going on with the two of them. Molly was always pretty outgoing; she was happy to see new people. Sometimes she'd be good around other dogs; sometimes she'd get snappy. Kiera, on the other hand, had started to become shy with both people and dogs. Molly's territorializing at home was noticeably affecting Kiera's personality and behaviors. This was not the playful, happy-go-lucky Kiera of a month ago.

Overall, Molly seemed to still be okay with her social skills. So, for as much time as I spent in town with Molly, I began spending more time in town with Kiera. We'd walk up and down the main street a couple of times. Then we'd go find one of the sidewalk benches to sit on and watch the world go by. It wouldn't take long before people would start coming over to tell me what a beauty Kiera was, and then invariably they'd ask what breed. Before I'd answer, I'd explain that Kiera was in training, and it would help her if they didn't try to reach down to pet her. This staved off most dog lovers' natural reactions of wanting to touch a dog. Then I'd keep my eyes on Kiera the whole time and treat her for any relaxed behavior. I wanted her to make the connection that people coming up meant tasty treats. It wasn't long before she started responding much better. I wasn't having the same luck getting her to feel safe around other dogs. That was going to take some time.

A whole week went by without any significant outbursts. I was starting to feel that I could take a deep breath again. Even Cait seemed to be gaining back some of her confidence, at least with Kiera. She'd decided that Kiera was the underdog and felt sorry for her. Kiera lapped up the attention and began following Cait around like a shadow, which made Cait feel very important. This freed me to feel better about giving Molly the lion's share of the attention.

If this was how it was going to be, I could live with it. It wouldn't be the same as if I were able to lavish all the love I felt for Kiera, but at least she was in my life. I'd look Kiera in the eye and tell her I was sorry for letting this happen, but that at least we were together and I loved her madly. She'd look back at me with those quiet, calm eyes as though to reassure me that she understood. Even though this arrangement wouldn't have been my first choice, when I'd agreed to take Molly, I hadn't done so lightly. Just because I'd been naive about the possible conse-quences of throwing two siblings together, I wasn't going to make Molly pay for that.

All in all, it seemed, we were finally getting it worked out. I let myself be lulled by the calm. It was the calm before the storm.

○

We were well into March and the beginning of mud season. I'd gone outside to get the mail and hadn't crated the dogs. I heard Cait screaming and crying inside the house. My blood drained. I flew back to the front door just as Cait was swinging it open to meet me. She grabbed onto me with a death grip, sobbing. I quickly checked her over to make sure she was okay. I asked what happened. She couldn't talk; shaking, she just pointed inside. I peeled her off me, told her to stay outside, and I went in.

This time, it was the real deal; Kiera and Molly meant business. They were in the throes of a "take no prisoners" fight. Enough of their adult teeth had come in so that they were able to rip into each other. There was no loud growling, no displays. I was looking at the silent fighting that Theresa had warned me about.

There was no time to think. I dove into the middle of them and took a bite to my ankle. Luckily, I had insulated boots on. I grabbed their collars, dragged them to their crates, and locked them in. I could tell from the flecks of blood on their coats that they'd landed a few good bites. They both lay down and started licking themselves. I'd deal with all of that in a minute. I spun around and saw Cait's little face, with tears streaming down, plastered to the glass on the front door. She'd been watching the whole time. I ran out and hugged her and reassured her until her sobbing stopped.

"I hate them, Mommy!" she cried. "I wish they never came."

I hugged her more tightly and stroked her head, "I know, honey. I know."

At that very moment, I couldn't help feeling the same way. I was starting to feel terrorized in my own home. There had been twenty-seven fights. I'd kept count the way a fighter pilot kept count of his missions, each bringing him closer to the last, until he'd finally be allowed go home in one piece. I wanted to go home in one piece.

That Cait had been witness to this last bloody encounter was the breaking point.

This was going to stop. And stop right now. I could feel something in me shut down. I'd been turned into a nervous wreck and I wasn't willing to live with this stress any longer. I was left with no choice. Even if I were willing to keep both dogs and have one crated or kept apart all the time, the risk of someone eventually winding up on the wrong side of a door was too great. One of the dogs had to go.

I'd finally thought the unthinkable. Now, how would I make the decision about who stayed and who went?

PART 3

Cheryl

CHAPTER 6

Rescued

NONE OF THE wounds required stitching. There were just a few punctures and a couple of small, shallow gashes. My EMT training came in handy. In a leaden stupor, I finished cleaning and dressing each dog's injuries and then recrated them, the whole time contemplating how I could possibly give either one of them up. I'd never had to give away one of my dogs before, and the thought thoroughly depressed me. It went against everything in my nature. On the other hand, I knew I could not survive one more fight. And I wasn't sure that my dogs would, either. But more importantly, I would not let Cait be traumatized any further. The die was cast.

I didn't see how I could give Molly away. What would be the odds of finding someone who would be willing to deal with her special needs? Granted, she was dazzlingly gorgeous, with her striking white-and-black silk coat and her humanlike blue eyes. But her looks could act as both a help and hindrance. Someone might be so taken with her beauty that they'd want her on the spot without considering all that was involved in learning how to communicate with her, while doing what was necessary to keep her safe. If someone actually thought it all through, which I'd make sure they did, they'd quickly realize how daunting it was.

Hands down, it would be easier to find a good home for Kiera. She was a classic-looking, pretty Aussie, with a good temperament. She was well trained and eager to keep learning. And she was full of love, just waiting for a chance to bestow it all on somebody. Maybe I'd be able to find a family that would get her involved in agility or herding, something I hadn't had time to try with her, even though she'd demonstrated natural abilities for both. She was an incredible athlete with a very sharp intelligence.

Unless the dogs were directly bothering Andrew, he usually didn't have much to say about them. He viewed them as mine, and therefore my responsibility. But this time I really needed his input; I asked him what he thought. Andrew was relieved that I'd decided to act on what, to him, was the obvious and only solution to the problem. It was my thought of having Kiera be the one to go that shocked him.

"You're seriously considering giving Kiera away?" he asked in disbelief, leaning against the kitchen counter.

"Well, what other option do I have, really?" I answered weakly, as I distractedly began tidying up.

"But we're talking about Kiera, the love of your life for as long as I've known you."

"You don't have to remind me." I covered my face and started crying.

He came over and pulled me into a hug. "Don't do this to yourself. You can find a home for Molly. You're not the only person in the world who would take on someone like Molly. It might take awhile, but there are others out there like you who would be just as good to her. You've said so yourself many times: Molly has a guardian angel. Put that angel to work one more time. I won't let you give Kiera away. That's not an option."

My throat was so tight I couldn't say anything. But I was profoundly thankful and relieved that Andrew had taken the burden of guilt off me, and had made the decision for me.

○

Now that another key decision had been made, I wanted to move the whole thing along as quickly as possible. I found it difficult to look at Molly without feeling sadness and remorse. She was being ousted because of something she couldn't help or change. In the meantime, I'd just keep giving her as much love as I could while I had her.

The next morning, I began working on how I would find a good home for Molly. I started by calling all my dog-savvy friends and asking them if they'd put the word out. I knew they'd screen any potential takers the same way I would. Then I snapped some pictures of Molly and made sure they all got a couple of photos.

Later that day, I made a visit to a woman who worked at a pet store not far from my vet's office. He'd recommended I talk to her about Aussies before I bought one, because she had a few. Of all the people I'd talked to during that time, she'd been the most thorough and honest in her assessment of life with Aussies. She'd stressed how crucial it was to socialize these dogs. And she had done me the favor of telling me exactly just how much exercise they really needed in order not to become obnoxiously nutty. Since she'd been so helpful once before, I thought she might be willing to be helpful again.

Boy was I wrong.

She blasted me. "You have a deaf dog who's aggressive with other dogs! Who would want her? All you do-gooders are alike. You take on these sad-sack cases, get into trouble, and then look for somewhere to dump your problems! I told you these were intense dogs! Did you think I was kidding? Nobody's going to want that dog. And I won't be a party to passing along your problem!"

I already felt bad enough. I didn't need a tongue lashing from someone who was so quick to condemn and who had no interest in knowing the full story.

I had to forcefully interrupt her steam roll. "Look, I'm not here for you to approve or disapprove of what I did. And I don't give a damn what you think of me. Whether you help me or not, I *will* find a good home for Molly."

I turned and started for the door.

As I put my hand on the doorknob, I heard her say, "Try the Aussie-L."

I swung around to look at her.

"It's an Australian Shepherd chat list on the Internet. There are some people on there who do rescue work."

"Thanks." I answered. "Thanks, very much."

○

I immediately went home, found the list, and figured out how to get subscribed. My first post explained my situation and asked if anyone knew of someone who might be able to help me out. I didn't have to wait long to get some responses.

What a cast of characters in "Aussie Land." There were a few who wrote scathing notes telling me I deserved what I got for not having Molly put down in the first place. One woman wrote to say that she had sixteen dogs and lived on Social Security, but she'd consider taking one more. A vet pointed me to some other Web sites on animal behavior and dog aggression to help me out until I could find a home for Molly. Most wrote to share helpful information about same-sex and sibling fights. There was a pretty disturbing suggestion, too: "Keep setting them up to fight, and then beat whichever dog started the fight with a stick until they stop."

That last example aside, it was evident that there were some very intelligent, knowledgeable, and helpful people on the list with whom I'd want to correspond. I wished I had known about this list at the beginning of my troubles. Eventually, I did hear from a woman involved in rescue who said she'd try to help me place Molly. But after that first e-mail, there was no further correspondence from her.

Every day I'd check my contacts like a fisherman checking his nets, hoping that I'd caught something—someone who could help, someone who knew someone, anything. In the meantime, I made sure one dog was crated at all times. It was the end of March and the weather would be getting warmer soon, and then I could keep one outside in a kennel. It was a job to keep track of who'd been where, for how long, and if they should be switched, and when the last time was they'd gone to the bathroom. It felt as if I were playing a shell game of sorts: Now you see this dog, now you don't; now you see that dog, now you don't.

Two weeks had gone by. Molly and Kiera's relationship wasn't improving any by the separation. It had gotten to a point where I needed to keep the crated dog in a different room with the door closed to keep them from growling and harassing each other all day.

The last thing I wanted to do was to put an ad in the paper, but I wasn't getting any bites anywhere else. It read: *Free to the right home. Special needs Aussie female, 6 mos old.* I figured, if nothing else, maybe it would stir the pot. And if there was one lesson I'd learned from Molly, it was to go full steam ahead and not look back. I just made my mind up that no matter what, I'd find a way to make this be a good thing for Molly.

I started getting calls right away. Hardly anyone was put off by Molly's deafness. But no one had the right setup I was looking for. Or they didn't have enough dog experience. Or something about them didn't sound right . . .

Andrew was home one evening when I got a call. After I'd hung up, he confronted me. "Do you put everyone who calls through that?"

"Through what?" I asked innocently.

"Through that grilling. You're trying to find a home for a dog, not your firstborn child."

"Very funny."

"No, I mean it," he said. "You've made it impossible for anyone to fit your criteria."

"Look, it's bad enough I have to rehome Molly. I just want to make sure that wherever she goes next, it will be her final home. She can be a handful, even without being deaf. I don't want her to get bounced around."

The phone rang and I went to pick it up. It was another call for Molly. I began going down my list of questions. Andrew just threw up his hands and walked out of the room.

It quickly became apparent that this was a different kind of call. The woman at the other end very gently interrupted me to let me know that she was involved with Aussie rescue work, and she was calling to say she wanted to help me get Molly into the right home. She introduced herself as Cheryl Luciano and began explaining about Aussie rescue. Then she asked about Molly and wanted to know what was causing me to give her away.

My throat closed up and I couldn't talk.

"It's okay," Cheryl reassured me. "I know this must be hard for you. Take your time. I'm not in any hurry."

The relief I felt was indescribable. That someone would not rush to judge, and would show such compassion meant so much. The last few months had been a rough road.

We proceeded to have a lengthy conversation. I shared Molly's story and told Cheryl that I knew it probably wouldn't be easy to find the right home for her. And I wouldn't let Molly go unless I knew she was at least as well cared for as she was with me. Cheryl then shared some rescue stories where she'd successfully placed a few "unplaceable" dogs, by way of encouraging me that it wasn't hopeless. She ended the conversation by saying that she'd get right to work on at least getting Molly put into a good foster home until a permanent home could be found for her.

After I hung up with Cheryl, I called the paper to have the ad taken out. Then I went to find Molly, and snuggled with her until we both fell asleep.

○

A few days later, I got a call from a young woman named Tara. She said that Cheryl had given her my name and had asked her to call. She also asked me to share Molly's story. She listened patiently and then asked some questions about Molly's training and how I communicated with her. I filled her in on all the details. She complimented me on all the work I'd done with Molly.

Then she told me a little bit about herself. She said that she was in her early twenties, and that she had been left legally deaf from an illness, and she could not hear without a hearing aid. She thought she and Molly shared a special kinship, and she would be willing to try fostering Molly. If it worked out, she would keep Molly permanently. She had a horse farm and was home all day. Molly would spend her days with Tara and her other dog, running through her fenced-in fields.

I'd been floored by her tale and found myself silently overcome for her and for Molly—they shared quite a kinship indeed. Life was just too strange and wonderful for words sometimes. I thanked her profusely. She just giggled a sweet giggle and said she'd like to get back in touch with Cheryl to set up a time when they could come and evaluate Molly.

That weekend, I met Cheryl and Tara in person. Cheryl was an attractive woman in her late thirties, with delicate features and an easy smile. Tara was taller, but she looked as though she could have been Cheryl's sister.

I had Kiera crated upstairs so Tara could meet Molly without distractions. Molly was in the kitchen with Andrew, Cait, and me. As Tara and Cheryl came around the back of the house and started up the deck, Molly went over to the door to look out, though she'd had no cue to do so. She wiggled all over the two of them as soon as they came through the door.

After we'd all made introductions, Cheryl asked me to begin working with Molly so she could watch our interactions. Molly was happy to have an audience to show off for. Then Cheryl took over and conducted a few tests to further her evaluation. Finally, Tara tried working with Molly, who was, as always, very responsive. After the last sit, Molly couldn't contain herself any longer. She jumped up on Tara, full of enthusiasm. Tara couldn't help but laugh as she reached to pick Molly up and got a face bath for her trouble.

Cheryl gave me a little thumbs-up sign behind Tara's back. I felt both overjoyed and sad at the same time.

Cheryl then suggested that Tara get her dog out of the car to see how the two of them got along. I nervously reminded Cheryl about Molly fighting with Kiera. Cheryl was quick to point out that she didn't think Molly would have a problem with Tara's dog because they weren't from the same litter, and weren't the same age. Besides, she assured me, if Molly got fresh, Tara's female was bigger and older, and would just teach Molly some manners.

While Tara was getting her dog, Cheryl nonchalantly handed me a little object that, when pressed, made a cricketlike sound. She'd noticed that I was using positive training and explained that what I was basically doing was clicker training without the clicker. She added that this "clicker," used as a marker, would help me in working with Kiera.

Tara had gotten her very large German Shepherd out of her car and brought her over. I put Molly on a leash and went into the backyard. They tentatively sniffed each other's noses. Molly started licking the German Shepherd's face, made a play bow, and tried to engage her in play. The Shepherd wagged her tail and made a little rushing motion at Molly, who dashed away and immediately came back and play-bowed again. Tara and Cheryl looked at each other and smiled.

Tara looked over at me and said, "Looks like Molly's found a new home."

I just stood there awkwardly, keeping my eyes on Molly.

Cheryl, always the helpful facilitator, suggested that Tara put her dog back in the car, and that I collect whatever things of Molly's I wanted to give to Tara.

As we walked back into the kitchen, Cheryl asked Cait if she was sad to see Molly go. Without batting an eye, Cait answered with a curt "No." I went to gather Molly's bedding, toys, leashes, and deaf dog books.

I'd managed to hold it all together until Cheryl suggested that I get an article of clothing of mine that Molly could have to snuggle and comfort herself with while she got used to her new surroundings. I became completely undone. Cheryl came over and gave me a big hug, telling me over and over that this was the right thing for my family and for Molly.

By this time, Tara had returned and lifted Molly up into her arms, where Molly nestled right in. Cheryl asked me if I wanted a few minutes alone with Molly before they left. I smiled weakly and explained that I'd had a feeling that once Tara and Molly met, it would be a done deal, so I'd already said my good-byes to Molly earlier. Saying good-bye again would only make it harder. Cheryl nodded that she understood.

Without further ado, I watched Tara and Molly walk out the door, with Andrew following behind, carrying all of Molly's things. Cheryl promised that she'd call in a few days to let me know how Molly was doing, and left me her phone number, encouraging me to call her if I needed to talk.

Molly's guardian angel had come through with flying colors one more time.

And in losing Molly, I'd gained a very special friend. Cheryl's role in my life was far from over.

CHAPTER 7

Me and My Shadow

MOLLY HAD BEEN gone for a week. Cheryl kept her promise and called a couple of days after Tara took Molly to let me know she was doing fine. Tara called a few days after that with glowing reports of how well Molly was getting along with her German Shepherd, and how she'd already bonded with Tara. She wanted to let me know she'd decided to keep Molly for good, rather than foster her until another home came along. Given all the odds, Molly was one lucky dog.

Tara also invited me to come visit Molly anytime I wanted. She was only an hour south of me. I thanked her and said that I'd like to take her up on that offer sometime. What I didn't tell her was that I didn't think it would be anytime soon.

Kiera and I both seemed to be in the grip of some kind of post-traumatic stress. Kiera manifested it mostly as lethargy, disinterest, and a pressing need to be in close physical contact with me at all times, as though, now that she had me again, she wasn't about to let anything come between us. For me, any sudden loud noise—a door slamming, the phone ringing, Cait dropping something—would send me into a momentary panic. I figured it was going to take a little while to decompress. As much as I loved Molly, I was happy to have my life back, such as it was.

○

April rolled around, the snow was finally gone, and the days were getting warmer. Work was picking up, so some days I needed to be at the office longer. On those days, I'd pick up Cait from school, we'd grab some lunch, and then I'd bring her back to the office with me for an hour or two. She'd sit at her little desk next to mine, play with all her art supplies, and mostly be contented. But most often, we were able to get home by noon. Kiera would be faithfully waiting by the door, wiggling her excitement.

Without the constraints of needing to keep one dog on a leash every time we went outside, a world of possibilities began to open up for us. But one of the issues that quickly became apparent was that Kiera and I hadn't had a chance to develop a way to play together yet. I tried throwing a ball for her. She'd halfheartedly start after it, stop, look at me, and come trotting back. I tried a Frisbee with only slightly better results: Sometimes she'd make it all the way to the Frisbee before she'd turn back. The only things she showed any interest in were our walks and training. Anything else I tried was a bust.

Figuring maybe it was an Aussie thing, I went back to the Aussie-L and asked for suggestions. I got several responses asking if I'd tried agility, or fly ball, or obedience. Another reminded me that Aussies liked a job, and would I consider training her for herding. These strategies resonated with what I was seeing in Kiera. She liked to learn and use her brain, and she liked to be near me. I decided I'd look into agility.

I found a teacher who lived a town over and who was very well regarded. She sent me a form asking about Kiera's temperament, background, and knowledge of commands. As I listed all of the words Kiera knew, I was amazed at how much ground we'd covered already. The hitch came when I saw that the recommendation was for dogs to be eight months to one year old before commencing training. As agility was a rather rigorous sport, it was considered better to start dogs after their bone growth was completed. Kiera had a few more months to go. And it seemed from our ball-throwing experience that fly ball would be an unlikely fit.

I called Cheryl to see if she knew of any herding events Kiera and I could go watch, to see if it looked like something I could ever get into. She not only located a herding trial, but offered to go with me. That Saturday, she and I drove an hour northeast to the Vermont border. She'd brought along one of her own rescued Aussies, a big old boy named Bear (one of her seven dogs at the time). I, of course, had Kiera.

We spent a chilly morning in a farmer's field watching a lineup of Aussies being put through their paces on both ducks and sheep. It was fascinating to observe, and easy to tell who'd been at it a long time. Those human–dog teams were like old married couples who hardly needed to look at each other to know what the other one was about to do. There were few surprises as they masterfully maneuvered the flock through various gates. The newer teams were just as much fun to watch for different reasons. Their lines of communication weren't quite as grooved, making what happened more unpredictable and, on occasion, downright funny.

Like this one Aussie who tried so hard to behave himself and do his job, when what he really wanted to do was eat a duck, any duck. You could see his prey drive start to kick in as he'd suddenly go from herding to stalking. His trainer would yell out to him. He'd get a grip on himself and pull himself back together—but then he couldn't help it; he'd go right back to stalking again, scattering his charges in ten different directions. He did finally manage to get most of the ducks through the course amid much flapping and quacking. A burst of loud cheers and laughter erupted when he finally got them through the last gate.

Well—maybe you had to be there.

After a few hours, Cheryl and I agreed we'd seen enough and decided to go somewhere to get a cup of coffee and thaw out. We stopped at a diner and sat by a window so we could keep a close eye on our dogs.

In the short time I'd known Cheryl, I'd observed that she wasn't one to shield herself from the hardships of life, with animals or with people. And yet she was able to remain unusually emotionally present. I couldn't imagine how she coped with the constant challenge and sadness that was just part of the deal for anyone doing rescue work. Holding my cold hands around the steaming cup, I asked Cheryl how she'd gotten into rescue.

She explained that some of it was simply an extension of working for a veterinarian; it was all rolled up in her love for animals.

When I asked her how she got involved with Aussie rescue in particular, the fuller story came out. About a decade ago, Cheryl's neighbor had an old Aussie girl who used to come over to Cheryl's house all the time. Cheryl fell in love with her. She decided that when she was ready, she'd get herself an Aussie. Not long after, she found a beautiful little male puppy she named Cooper. This little Aussie became the love of Cheryl's life and they bonded with the power of superglue.

All was well until it came time to have Cooper neutered. For some reason, Cheryl didn't want to have the procedure done on the dog. She just had a bad feeling about it. But she couldn't put her finger on why. Wanting to do the responsible thing, she finally let reason overrule her gut and went ahead with it. The surgery was uneventful and her boy came home. But that night, Cheryl could see that something was definitely wrong; the dog's lips had turned pale. By morning, he was weak and going into shock. She rushed him to the vet's, but it was too late. She would later discover that her beloved dog was a hemophiliac and had internally bled to death. To say that this was a life-altering event for Cheryl would be an understatement. Its ramifications would ripple through her life for years to come—not the least of it being the beginning of her rescue work with Aussies.

On the drive home, I thought about the path Cooper had sent Cheryl down, and wondered how many dogs had been saved in honor of his name. I also thought about what a strong heart it took to do what Cheryl was doing. She was one of those people who walked her talk without any fanfare.

○

Later that evening, I decided to check in with the Aussie-L to ask a few questions about what was involved in getting started with herding. I knew quite a few of the members on the list had working farms and working dogs, and would be full of helpful tips.

From reading the latest posts, I could see that there was a discussion of tail docking in progress. Even though I knew this was a gathering place of fanatics, I imprudently decided to put my two cents in anyway. And because I wasn't considered a fanatic about Australian Shepherds, or competition, or trials, or obedience for that matter, just fanatically in love with my dog, right away I was considered something of a lightweight. Then I really set myself apart when I wrote that I thought docking Aussies' tails, or any dogs' tails, was unnecessary and inhumane treatment.

This same group that had appeared friendly and helpful on other occasions seemed to turn on me in unison, as if to say, *Them's fightin' words*. The argument that ensued turned into a knock-down, drag-out free-for-all. By this time, I'd jumped in with both feet and wasn't about to accept being beaten back from my position, because it was a subject I happened to feel pretty strongly about.

My contention was that a dog's tail aided in its balance, and was a major component in its communication. Without it, dogs were at a distinct disadvantage, at the very least, with other dogs. In most cases, there was no health reason to prompt removing a dog's tail. This had just become a fashion thing— somebody decided a long time ago that Aussies looked better without tails. I wondered if it was possible to think independently about this without defending what had been, out of habit, but to really think new thoughts about what it meant to do this to our dogs?

Most answered with a resounding *"No!"*

In essence, their argument was that I had no right to question the AKC breed standards. This was how the breed was supposed to look, and if I didn't like it, I should go get myself a dog with a tail and leave them alone.

After several rather vituperative volleys, it became evident this was going to be a fruitless conversation, with no way of getting things back on an even keel. The rancorous feelings lingered long after the "discussion" stopped. I realized now that most of this group wasn't really open to reflecting on any ideas that hadn't already met with their stamp of approval.

One good thing that came out of that encounter was that it started me examining areas of my own life where I might have blinders on. In what ways had I bought into a party line a long time ago, and never bothered to reexamine how I really felt? It was an exercise that reminded me of just how difficult it was to be open-minded when you felt that you had something you wanted to protect.

In the process, I managed to find and air out some stale and stagnant places in my thinking, and to let go of some old sacred cows. For that I was appreciative, though I decided to keep any future conversations on the "L" purely to subjects where I was looking for help with Kiera.

○

The next morning, after my close encounter on the "L," I was cleaning around the kitchen and found the clicker Cheryl had left me. I picked it up and clicked it a few times to see if I could figure out how this thing might work in conjunction with training. Kiera cocked her head at the sound and came over to sniff it. Every time I clicked it, she'd look over. It definitely worked as an attention-getter. I decided to go to the bookstore to see if I could find a book that would teach me about clicker training.

I came home with a couple of books and dove right in. One of the first things I decided to try was to see if I could get Kiera a little more excited about playing ball with me. I was really looking for a way to get in extra exercise for Kiera on top of our walk/runs. I thought maybe if I could get her to run around more and play, that might also help lift her spirits.

With a book open on the table, I read as I went. The clicker was nothing more than a marker, I read. It was a means of letting the dog know exactly when it did something right, for which it could be expected to be rewarded. The click, then, became a way of being able to simultaneously identify and reinforce the desired behavior by letting the dog know exactly when it had accomplished what you were asking, and then be rewarded with food.

First, I had to "charge" the clicker, which meant I had to get Kiera to associate the clicker with getting a food reward. I did this by clicking and immediately offering Kiera a small piece of hot dog. I repeated this several times. The clicker was considered charged and ready to go when the dog looked for a treat as soon as the clicker was clicked. With my food-obsessed dog, this was not a long process.

I thought I'd try getting her to think that playing ball was as good as it gets. If I could get clicker training to work for that, then I'd know I was really on to something. I started by holding the ball in my hand. As soon as she came to sniff it, I clicked and treated. It wasn't long before she became a sniffing fool. Then I upped the ante: In order to get a click/treat now, she had to touch the ball with her nose. She figured it out pretty quickly — anything to get that piece of hot dog. Time to move the clicking game outside.

I started by lobbing the ball only a few feet away. This time, in order to get a click/treat she only had to look over at the ball. I built up the steps from there, until, incrementally, she learned to run after the ball herself, pick it up, bring it back, and drop it at my feet.

I learned early on that the secret to success with clicker training was not to lump any steps together. It was important to be careful to break each task I wanted Kiera to learn into step-by-step building blocks (called "criteria" in clicker training lingo). I wouldn't move on to the next criterion until Kiera was reliably performing the previous criterion a very high percentage of the time. I could always tell when I was trying to move her along too rapidly, because she'd start sliding backward and get confused. That was my cue to back it up to where it was easy for her and then go forward with each step a little more slowly.

The most amazing thing to watch was how the whole process of clicker training got Kiera to actually think about and anticipate what it was I was asking her to do. Her alertness and attention span were unbelievable. She was intensely focused anytime we'd start to work, and highly motivated to find the shortest distance between figuring out what I wanted her to do and getting the food reward. I felt as if I could actually watch the gears in her brain work. If you haven't experienced this, it's something you'd have to see to believe.

It only took a few days to have her racing after that ball as if it were a T-bone steak. And only a few more days to run out and catch Frisbees with a joie de vivre in midair leaps. Within a week, my girl was off and running—literally. It was a major development for both of us in recovering a sense of light-hearted play.

Kiera and I were finally growing strongly together. We were catching up on lost time, cementing the bond that would hold us together.

CHAPTER 8

Rescued Again

IT WAS NOW the beginning of May, and getting to be that time of year when I'd start preparing my vegetable garden for planting. Cait had her own set of garden tools and liked to get all the planting rows ready. Kiera, on the other hand, loved to help me work in the compost. I'd throw a few shovelfuls on each section of raised bed, and Kiera would vigorously scratch it in with her front paws, sending the dirt flying through her back legs, every once in a while suddenly stopping to stick her nose in the rich mixture, snort, and then start furiously digging again. This would send Cait into peals of laughter, which only seemed to egg Kiera on.

When we were all done, we'd go inside, wash our hands, and then grab Kiera's leash and Cait's helmet. While I walked Kiera, Cait would ride her bike next to me. This way, we could go a few miles without Cait getting tired.

By the time we got back, it'd be time for me to get dinner started. Cait would take Kiera back outside and play tag or throw a ball or Frisbee. It was a perfect arrangement. Both my girls would be thoroughly exhausted by bedtime, and usually nod right off. And Andrew and I would get to have some quiet time together before it would start all over again the next day.

○

One morning at work, I found an e-mail from Cheryl waiting for me. Figuring there was another chance for us to get together, I immediately opened it. It read:

> Hi Karen,
> I know your life feels pretty balanced right now, so feel free to pass. But if you thought you had room for another dog, there's a little black English Shepherd mix that I think would be perfect for you. His picture is on our CAPP (Companion Animal Placement Program) Web site.
> Cheryl

I stiffened as I read the contents. It wasn't that I didn't want to consider another dog in need. Given what Cheryl had done for me with Molly, if there was any way I could have helped her rehome another rescue dog, I would have. And if I had lived by myself, I would have loved to get another dog for both Kiera and me. But I didn't live by myself. And after what we'd all been through with Molly, I couldn't imagine asking Andrew to agree to another dog. I wouldn't let myself think about it for another moment. Without a further thought, I sent Cheryl back this e-mail:

> Hi Cheryl,
> Thanks for thinking of me. I wish I could help out, but things have been pretty calm, and I don't feel that I could ask Andrew to go for another dog. Maybe someday, but not right now.
> Karen

I knew Cheryl would understand and wouldn't take it personally. I also knew she couldn't help asking, because she'd try every last option for any dog in need of a home. It was one of the things that made her so special. I'd secretly dubbed her the patron saint of dogs in need. I put the whole thing out of my head, finished my work, and went to pick up Cait.

○

That night, I was startled awake by the eerie cries of what sounded like some kind of wild dogs. Their yips, trills, and yodels gave me the creeps and sent Kiera into skittish pacing and whining in between episodes of pawing at the door to get out. I remembered that Andrew said he'd seen what he thought was a coydog a few nights before on his way home from work. Now this. I didn't like the idea of a pack of wild dogs slinking through our woods while Cait might be playing in the yard.

There was no way I could tell from their peculiar barking how many they were, so I went downstairs to get my binoculars to see if I could get a look at them. Their calls were coming from what sounded like the hill on the far side of our yard. It was one of those full moons that bathed the earth in a soft glow. I focused on the ridge behind a row of trees beyond our pond, where I thought I could see several shapes gathered.

I involuntarily took a step back as I dropped the binoculars from my eyes and then hurriedly put them back up to make sure my eyes weren't playing tricks. They weren't. I was looking at five coyotes sitting in a jagged row, noses pointing up while they sang in rounds.

When they abruptly stopped, they appeared to be looking right back at me. Unnerved, I lowered the binoculars to break their gaze. I was filled with the very weird but strong sensation that they'd come to tell me something. Thinking that was a rather strange thought, I shook myself and decided it was just my overactive imagination at work. I looked through the binoculars again. They were gone.

I went back to bed and lay awake staring at the ceiling. I was aware that coyotes had made it into the Adirondacks awhile back, but I found it disconcerting that they'd already traveled down into our neck of the woods. It was going to be one more thing to worry about, along with the fishers (fierce weasels) in the back of our property, and that mountain lion I'd spotted lapping out of our pond the previous summer. We lived only a couple of miles outside of a small city, half an hour north of Albany in upstate New York, yet it felt as though we were living in the midst of a wild kingdom.

This new twist conspired against any sleep. So rather than just lie there, I decided to get up and do some writing. I quietly padded to the little alcove off our bedroom where my office was set up. Kiera moved silently with me and curled up around my feet as soon as I sat down. I turned on the computer and listened to the familiar whir as the hard drive booted. Instead of opening the document I'd planned to work on, I found myself at the CAPP Web site.

"I'll just take a look," I told myself. No harm in that.

I found the link that brought up the photos of dogs available for adoption. I scrolled down the pictures, of which there were several—always a surplus of needy dogs. I looked at each picture. There were a couple of Lab mixes, a Shar-Pei mix, a Rottweiler. There were a couple of indeterminate black mixes. I stopped on one of a little black dog who looked so sweet and so scared at the same time that my heart immediately went out to him. The name above his picture read MAGIC. Something about him caught me. As I read his description, I realized this was the dog Cheryl had been talking about. Interesting.

"Don't do this," I told myself. "Shut this computer off right now."

I got up and went downstairs again, this time to get a glass of water, muttering to myself the whole way. "First of all, he's a boy. I don't want a male dog; they pee on everything." I got my water and paced around the kitchen table. "Second of all, Andrew would kill me, absolutely kill me."

I started back upstairs. Kiera was right by my side. I reached over on the step and scratched her head. "And what would you make of him, huh, girl?" I asked.

I started to walk by my desk, fully intending to go back to bed. I got three steps past, did an about-face, turned the computer back on, and immediately went back to studying Magic's picture. The adjoining information box let me know that he was approximately six months old (same age as Kiera) and had been surrendered by a family. The description continued: sweet, friendly, good with other dogs.

I can't explain it, but something about him struck a chord; I couldn't take my eyes off him. And it wasn't because I felt sorry for him. At other times in my life when I'd been looking for a dog, the first place I always started looking was the shelters. I'd always had good luck with finding cats at shelters, but not so much with dogs; only two of my dogs (a Sheltie and a Shepherd mix who came as a package deal) had come from a shelter. As badly as I wanted to give all those other dogs a home, I knew I'd be taking them for the wrong reason—because I felt sorry for them, not because I felt a connection to them.

Something else was going on with this dog named Magic. Something that compelled me to dash off an e-mail to Cheryl in the middle of the night. It read:

Cheryl,
I did a bad thing. I looked at Magic's picture and now I can't get him out of my mind. If I can get Andrew to agree to it, can you arrange for me to meet him to have a look? I'm going back to bed now, and hopefully I'll get some sleep.
Karen

I shut off the computer, went to bed, and slept soundly through the rest of the night.

I found this e-mail in my inbox first thing at the office.

LOL. How about this weekend? You name the time, I'll find the place.
Cheryl

I felt both excited and petrified. It was crazy that I hadn't even seen this dog in person, and I knew I loved him. How was I going to find the courage to bring this up with Andrew? He'd tell me I needed to have my head examined.

It took me two days to muster up the mettle to approach Andrew. In my usual inimitable style, I finally just walked into his office and blurted it all out.

"Let me get this straight," Andrew summarized. "Cheryl has found a dog who would be a great fit for our family, and he'd be a good friend for Kiera, because he's a male? And you want me to go have a look at him with you?"

"Um, yeah." Watching Andrew rub his brow, I quickly assured him, "You'd get to have the final verdict." I stood nervously in front of his desk, hands jammed into my pockets, rocking back on my heels.

I would not have been surprised if he'd said that sometimes he wondered why he ever married me, because I was certifiably loony. I mean, how many times was I going to put this man through this?

He paused for several moments before he began. "You and Cheryl are a dangerous combination . . ."

Assuming a "nay" in the making, I quickly felt deflated.

Then he finished his thought. "Okay. But we're just going to have a look."

I screamed and dove over the desk to give him a hug.

O

Andrew and I chatted about everything except dogs on the way to the pet store, where Cheryl had agreed to meet us. Cait and Kiera were cuddling in the backseat. They were an important part of this decision. Much of this depended on how they both did with Magic.

As we pulled in, I could already see Cheryl's car in the parking lot. I clicked the leash on Kiera and got out of the car. Andrew held open the store door and we all went in.

Cheryl was trying to contain this little bundle of ribs and muscle. Except for tan socks and a small white diamond on his chest, he was cloaked in black. A scrawny, feral-looking thing, he topped out at thirty-five pounds—some kind of English Shepherd–mutt mix by anybody's best guess. He was busy straining against the leash, sniffing at everything in sight. Cheryl looked up and smiled, handed the leash to the store manager, and came over to give us all a warm hug, including Kiera.

"Well, there he is. What do you think?" she asked, sweeping her hand toward him.

I had mixed emotions. Standing there in the flesh, I didn't feel the same thing for him that I had when looking at his picture. I didn't know what to make of anything at that point.

I handed Kiera to Andrew and went over closer to him. I just watched him for a few moments. He seemed a little high-strung, and completely disinterested in all of us, including Kiera. I didn't realize at the time that this behavior was normal for a dog who hadn't been well socialized.

Cheryl, seeming to read my mind, said, "It's been awhile since he's seen anything except the inside of a crate. The woman who's fostering him works all day, so he spends most of his time cooped up. I don't think he knows what to do with all this freedom in a new place with so many smells."

I knelt down and extended my hand for him to sniff. He immediately looked up at me and began licking my hand. I scratched him behind an ear and he rested his head on my knee, half closing his eyes in contentment.

I still wasn't sure. He looked half starved; he was so skinny.

I asked Cheryl if there was someplace we could take the two dogs and let them off-leash to see how they did together. She asked the store manager if we could use the fenced-in yard next door. The woman graciously obliged.

Once the dogs were safely inside the enclosed yard, and the gate was latched behind us, we let them free. Magic, still disinterested in all of us, went off to sniff and pee on the flower garden. Kiera stayed pressed up against my leg just watching him.

Cheryl, noticing the strained look on my face, told me to give them a few minutes to get used to each other. She clapped her hands for Magic to come, and he came trotting over. Kiera, seeing him come toward her, dashed out to meet him. Her body stiffened and she held her head high. I held my breath.

Then, before I could blink, they exploded into rapturous play. We all laughed and clapped. First Kiera was herding Magic, flanking him within inches of his side, as they flashed by in a blur. Then Magic whirled about, and the chased became the chaser. Then they switched. Then Kiera. Then Magic. Then Kiera. It was as if they were floating together in a dance that only they knew the steps to. Even Andrew was smiling.

I looked at Andrew with raised eyebrows, as if to say, *Yes?*

He just shrugged and nodded yes.

I looked at Cait.

She took my hand, looked up at me, and said, "Mommy, Kiera's found a husband."

I walked over to Cheryl and began asking her questions in earnest. I wanted to know why that family had given Magic up.

She told me what history she knew. Apparently, it was a family that never had a dog before. There were two young boys who had gotten into the habit of handling Magic a little too roughly. According to the mother, Magic, in self-defense, had nipped one of the boys. That, and the fact that the mother didn't want to deal with all that was involved with a puppy, pretty much doomed his chances with them.

"Cheryl," I said. "*Nipping* and *children* are not two words I want to hear in the same sentence."

"I know," she answered. "And if I thought there was a smidgen of danger to Cait, you know I would never suggest this dog for you. He's been thoroughly evaluated and tested, and has never been anything except sweet and gentle. I really do believe those boys were more than just a little rough."

I let out a deep sigh. I didn't want another problem.

Just then, Magic went over to Cait and began licking her hand. She grabbed him around his neck and gave him a big bear hug. He just wagged his tail and licked her face. Then Kiera ran over and hijacked him for another relay race.

Andrew had heard what Cheryl had said. I looked over and asked his opinion.

"This is your call," he said.

I looked back at Cheryl. "Can we take him home overnight and see how it works out?"

"Sure," she answered. "If it doesn't work out, I'll come and pick him up."

I let out another deep sigh. "Okay, let's see how it goes."

We put Kiera in the backseat with Cait, and I held Magic on my lap in front. He immediately snuggled against my body, made himself comfortable, and fell fast asleep. It was only then that I felt that same feeling that I'd felt looking at his picture. I knew in that moment that he wasn't going back, that he'd found his home. But I kept that thought to myself.

PART 4
Magic

CHAPTER 9

Halcyon Days

I CARRIED MAGIC into our backyard and gently lowered him down. He hugged the back of the house, unwilling to venture away from safety. Andrew, Cait, and I sat on the deck to be unobtrusively near. It wasn't hard to imagine that, for a six-month-old puppy who'd been crated for much of the past two months, this kind of freedom and open space would seem overwhelming. As much as I wanted to go over and cuddle him, I knew that would only reinforce his anxiety. I didn't want to do that. It'd be better to let him come around on his own time. I could wait. After all, I'd have him for the rest of his life.

As much as I could tell that Kiera was anxious for him to play with her again, the way he had that morning, she was endearingly gentle. She patiently stood nearby without crowding him. It was as though she could tell he needed to be allowed to get his bearings in these unfamiliar surroundings. She'd occasionally go over and lick his face, and he'd offer a quick lick back. They seemed to be holding their own private conversation, conducted in sniffs, licks, and nuzzles.

I got up to go over and watch them. Magic suddenly stiffened, bringing himself up to his full height. He looked at me, and then at Kiera. He play-bowed, stretched out his skinny bowlegged back legs one at a time, and then started zigging and zagging around the yard at breakneck speeds, navigating an obstacle course only he could see. After he'd sprinted through his imaginary agility course, he began tracing wide arcing circles around us. I knelt down and stretched my arms out to him. He came scooting in, tail wagging, and leapt into my arms to happily lick my face. I couldn't stop laughing.

Finally, Kiera pushed him off me and teased him back into play. Once again, my two energetic acrobats were zooming around doing leaps and twirls over and around each other. Cait was so happy for Kiera that she jumped up and down, clapping her hands in delight. When Magic strayed too far, Kiera would herd him back closer to the house; she was already beginning to teach him the boundaries. It was heartening to watch, and as joyful a day I'd had in a long while. The sun drenched us in its warmth, Andrew and Cait were near, Kiera was happy, and I had another dog to love.

○

Magic eased into our life as though he'd always been a part of it. He quickly picked his spots for lying down, and hungrily gobbled up affection. He was so thankful for any food, and so openly grateful for any kindness, that it was if he were constantly singing out, I'm so happy to be alive! He even won Andrew over. And he'd captured my heart as completely as had Kiera. It appeared Cait was right, Kiera had found a husband; the two of them quickly became lovingly inseparable. It seemed a match truly made in Heaven for all of us.

I began working with Magic right away. I knew his foster mom had taught him a few commands in what little time she had with him, but he still had a ways to go. He was smart and eager to do anything that made me happy, so he caught on quickly. Having Kiera right there showing him the ropes seemed to help. Rather than getting confused by Kiera's presence when we were training, he seemed reassured to have her there. Whenever he wasn't sure what I was asking, he'd look to see what Kiera was doing. If she was sitting and looking at me, he'd try sitting to see if that's what I wanted.

While I was getting Magic set up with the basic commands, I was also working on house training. I'd been worried about him needing to mark everything in sight, but he hadn't once lifted his leg in the house. I approached house training in my usual way, staying on top of it really intensively for several days. I knew the more I could minimize accidents in the house, and reward going outside, the quicker a dog would catch on. Magic was no exception. He had one accident inside and that was it.

I was also beginning to discover that Magic was a bit of a ham. He'd bring Kiera a stick and lay it daintily at her feet, as though it were a gift as valuable as the queen's jewels. Just as she'd bend her head to pick it up, he'd snatch it and go screaming around the yard, doing his version of a cackling hyena. Kiera would ignore him for being such a big brute, and for treating her so badly. He'd become contrite and go over to her to make up, forgetting, it seemed, that he still had the coveted stick in his mouth. Just as he'd drop it to kiss and make up, Kiera would nab it and streak off, sending a doggy refrain of *Nah, nah, na, nah, nah!* The two of them were a couple of regular cut-ups together. They filled my days with lighthearted laughter.

Nights were another matter. Kiera (now seven months) had been able to make it until dawn, but Magic still needed to go out at least once in the middle of the night, usually around 1 A.M. Though tiring, this round was a breeze compared with my recent winter stint. Magic was great about going right out and doing his business. He wasn't interested in sightseeing or playing. He wanted to be done as quickly as possible so he could nestle back into his blankets in his cozy crate, where he'd sleep soundly again until 5 A.M.

O

About a week after we'd gotten Magic, Andrew casually asked at breakfast one morning if I'd mentioned to my mother yet that I'd gotten another dog. I hadn't. My mother had had a front-row seat during the Molly Chronicles, so I knew she'd be less than thrilled to hear about Magic. I was avoiding the inevitable disapproval I knew would be forthcoming. But Andrew was right. It was time to get the news over with.

I'd always been close to my mother, but since my father died, I'd gotten into the habit of calling her several times a week. As much as I did this to check up on her, I did it to help reassure myself that, at least with my mother's presence still in the world, I could go on. During the week, we'd talked easily about everything, but I never found an opportune moment to bring up Magic.

Even with Andrew's prodding, it still took me a couple more days to address the matter. I decided the best way to share the news was in an e-mail. It didn't take long to get a response. I knew she couldn't help herself; she shot back an e-mail that essentially said she thought this was a big mistake and that I was looking for trouble just when my life was settling back down. I knew her comments were coming from a loving place so I didn't take offense. And I couldn't argue with her reasoning. But reasoning had nothing to do with it.

I wrote back:

Now, Mom, I know this doesn't make sense to you because you've never had to think about whether Asia [her ten-year-old German Shepherd] *is lonely or getting enough exercise. And the reason for that would be because Asia has always had Eric's and Rip's* [my brothers] *dogs around to keep her company and to get her to move her butt.*

My little Magic (he is little and that's his name) has already made my life easier. He and Kiera play all day until they're exhausted, and then they sleep the sleep of the dead. They are hysterical to watch (one can never underestimate the value of comic relief in these trying times) and Kiera is noticeably happier. This, in turn, allows me to be at work for longer periods of time without feeling guilty because Kiera's life stops until I get home. I think the problem now will be that she won't even notice I'm gone and I could start feeling a little jealous.

And you don't have to worry about me asking you to watch them if we ever go away. I've found a great kennel nearby where they play Frisbee with them and let them run together in a big fenced yard. But alas, for now, we won't be getting away anytime soon. Toodles for now.

My mother never said another word about my decision to keep Magic.

○

After three weeks, I heard Magic bark for the first time. Andrew and Cait were off to the library to get some new books, and Kiera and Magic were outside keeping me company while I worked in the yard. Kiera was lying near me, ignoring Magic's attempts to get her up to play with him. Finally, not knowing what else to do, he barked. Kiera and I both looked at him in surprise. He looked surprised too, as if to say, Who did that? Not me!

I looked at Kiera and said, "Well, what do you make of that, my girl? Magic finally feels safe enough to bark." She looked up at me and then cocked her head at Magic.

Excited by this breakthrough, I barked back at him and crouched into my version of a play bow, trying to get him to bark again. At first, he looked at me and pulled back a little with a startled expression. Then he barked right back and chased after me. We raced around the yard, yipping and running, until I collapsed with exhaustion on the grass. Both dogs piled on top of me, taking turns licking my face. I pulled them into my arms and scratched them all over. Magic lolled on his back and wagged his tail contentedly. It seemed he could finally really believe he wasn't going to be shipped off again; that this was his final home, a place where he could let it all hang out. It was as though I were watching Pygmalion's sculpture come to life. Each day after that, Magic would uncork a little bit more of his personality until his transformation was complete. What stood in place of the cowering, scared little puppy was a well-behaved, loving, and exuberant young dog.

○

Picking peas was a favorite early-summer ritual for Cait and me. And the first crop of snap peas was ready. We grabbed our baskets and raced each other back to the garden to see who could be the first to stuff those sweetly delicious peas into our mouths. Cait would always thrill at winning the race—and then accuse me of letting her win. In the past, that had been true, but not anymore. Cait was fast as lightning. She'd beaten me fair and square this time. I didn't point out that Magic and Kiera were actually the real winners. They'd blown right past us both.

Magic had discovered the succulent taste of peas all on his own a few days earlier. While keeping me company during one of my weeding sessions, he watched me munch on a pod and tried one. The taste agreed with him and so whenever he wanted a little snack, he'd jog back out there and help himself. That morning, he was eating peas off the vine faster than Cait and I could pick them, so we all just stood out there and ate as we picked. I don't think we got one pot of cooked peas that whole summer. It was always a contest for Cait and me to get back there and eat them raw before Magic would polish them off.

Kiera, on the other hand, had a more sophisticated palate. I'd just baked an apple pie and put it all the way back on the counter to cool, safely out of my counter-surfer's reach. I noticed that Kiera had bored of our pea-popping party rather quickly and had skulked back into the house. I didn't put two and two together.

When we walked back into the house fifteen minutes later, there was an empty pie plate—unmoved from the back of the counter—licked totally clean, without a crumb in sight. I actually had a moment where I thought Andrew had eaten the whole thing and then washed the pie plate for me. But I quickly realized that it couldn't have been my husband. There was no way he could have eaten that whole pie in one sitting. There really could only be one culprit, but my Aussie girl wasn't talking.

One question remained: Had Kiera actually managed to jump up on the counter (twice her height), or had she somehow snagged the plate, pulled it forward to eat, and then pushed it back into place when she was done? Since there were no crumbs anywhere, I was inclined to think that she had indeed negotiated the jump up. Unbelievable.

○

As the summer wore on, the dogs lost interest in our gardening activity and started going on mousing expeditions instead. They'd slowly stalk through the grass until they'd sniff out a mouse. Suddenly, with all four legs held stiffly, they'd hop up in the air and pounce on their prey. When they were in the tall grass, all I'd see was the back of one dog or the other boing-ing up and down like Tigger through the reeds. I never saw either one of them actually kill a mouse. It was just a game they played to amuse themselves on any given afternoon. Their other favorite pastime was to chomp on tadpoles they'd catch in the pond. But first they'd have to chase off a very miffed Great Blue Heron who'd claimed the pond as his own several years prior.

He was not pleased with these furry interlopers, but he wisely accepted that he was outnumbered.

Later that summer, Molly came to visit. Cheryl had been keeping me abreast of Molly's progress and mentioned that she and Tara were going to be up my way to help at a pet adoption clinic. They wanted to stop in to say hello. I knew Molly was thriving and happy with Tara, and enough time had passed so I was genuinely looking forward to seeing her again.

The dogs and I were outside when they turned into the driveway. I let Magic stay out because I knew he'd be happy to see Cheryl. And I let Kiera stay because I thought there was a chance that she'd be happy to see Molly. I was thinking that not all the time they'd spent together was bad. And there had only been good times since Molly's departure.

I went to give both Tara and Cheryl a hug. As soon as Molly hopped out of the car, Kiera started whining uncomfortably while pacing behind my legs. Magic, sensing that Kiera wasn't okay with Molly's presence, started barking and charging at Molly. He was trying to keep her from coming into the backyard.

Cheryl picked up on all of this right away. "So Magic has become Kiera's little protector, eh?" She reached down confidently to give him a pat.

"Looks like it," I answered, not having seen this behavior in Magic before.

Molly was being perfectly well mannered. She had no interest in Kiera, or Magic for that matter. She was just trying to get over to see me.

I suggested that I put Kiera and Magic in their crates so we could visit in peace. Both Tara and Cheryl nodded their agreement that this would be a good idea.

I collected the dogs and got them settled upstairs. Magic started whining when I put him in his crate, looking over at Kiera, who'd gone to the back of her crate and immediately lay down. I looked from him to her. He was agitated by her behavior, as though he knew that Molly's arrival had depressed her.

I spoke to Kiera in an encouraging tone. "Don't worry, my love. She's not coming to stay. I won't let anything happen to you. You have Magic and me to keep you safe. I won't let Molly ever come back to visit. You'll never have to see her again."

She wouldn't even look at me. I could see that Magic was bothered by her demeanor. He wanted to be right with her. To do what? I wondered. To reassure her? To reassure himself? Whatever it was, it was clear he needed to be with her, so I opened his door and put him in with her. Kiera lifted her head to look at him and he softly bathed her face. She contentedly closed her eyes and let Magic wash her. Then he circled around her and lay right next to her with his head resting across her back. They both seemed better.

I walked back downstairs feeling awful for having created this situation for Kiera. What made me think that Kiera would be happy to see Molly? I reproached myself for being such a Pollyanna, thinking I could make the world into one big happy place. As I stepped out on the deck, I put on a smile and concentrated on being with my two new friends and catching up on the news. Molly contentedly snuggled on my lap for most of the visit. I loved that Molly was so happy to see me and seemed to show no ill effects from being rehomed. In fact, she was doing visibly better with Tara than she had done with us. What were the chances that this could have all worked out so well? I appreciated how lucky Molly was, but also how lucky I was.

Tara and Cheryl were on a tight schedule and had to get back to the clinic, so they didn't stay long. I hugged them and silently said my last good-bye to Molly. This time I knew it was time for me to let her go for good.

○

They say life begins when the kids leave home and the dog dies.

For me, life started that fall when Cait entered kindergarten, and Magic started making it through the night until 6 A.M. And both the dogs had learned how to use the dog door.

These banner events all happened within a few days of each other. I was suddenly a free woman. In celebration, I took the day off from work, hung out in the backyard, and did nothing but read a book all day, with my two snugglers lying on my feet. They'd occasionally rouse themselves for a bracing game of tag or leapfrog, and then plunge themselves into the pond to cool off. Invariably, they'd wait to shake off until they were right next to me, and then drop their soggy bodies back down on my feet. I couldn't imagine a more pleasant way to pass the day.

I knew I should have spent part of the day socializing Magic, because it was getting to be a bit of a challenge to find the time to fit it in. But I didn't want to do work of any kind — not business work, not housework, not yard work, not even dog work. I just wanted to turn my brain and body off, and put everything on idle. And getting my two dogs into town and walking around while training was hardly relaxing.

My preference was to take each dog into town separately. But Magic, not surprisingly, had developed a case of separation anxiety. He'd gotten attached to me nearly instantaneously, and found it very stressful to have me out of his sight. I was prepared for this, having been through this experience once before with my Shepherd mix who came from a shelter. It all made perfect sense to me: What creature who'd been abused or abandoned, and then found peace and safety in another person, wouldn't be anxious when the source of his security went missing in action?

Within days of Magic's arrival, he took to shadowing me wherever I went, and as soon as I'd sit down, he'd use my foot for a pillow. He wouldn't let me out of his sight. To ward off an escalating case of separation anxiety, I had started working with

Magic right away. He'd made significant progress, with me being able to leave him home for longer and longer stretches of time, until I could leave him for a few hours. I accomplished this with a desensitization program. I'd leave for a few minutes at a time and then return, ignoring him on leaving and returning. As soon as he reverted to a relaxed state, I'd reward him with food and affection. It wasn't long before I could leave him contentedly with a peanut-butter-stuffed Kong and be gone indefinitely.

It was an entirely different matter when I tried to leave Magic and take Kiera into town to work with her. Again not surprisingly, he experienced this as double desertion and would become completely undone. I'd have to work with him incrementally again, this time with both Kiera and me leaving and returning. The short-term solution was to take him along, too, and figure out a way to work with them individually while they were together.

But in every other way, Magic was progressing perfectly. He was growing into a healthy, happy dog. He was my pride and joy, and Kiera's true love. Our first year together flew by in a blissful blur. Life couldn't have been better.

○

All was quiet. The clock showed 1:30 a.m. A little whimper came from the crate next to my bed. A soft padding sound approached. A wet nose nuzzled the crate door from the outside. Kachink, kachink went the latches. The crate door sprang open. Eight little feet pattered away to the dog bed by the window. Two happy bodies settled down on top of each other. Deep sighs. Quiet.

Kiera had rendered the final piece of Magic's past—being crated every night—obsolete. Magic, unfettered at last, finally and truly knew complete love and freedom.

CHAPTER 10

You Love Them More

I CAME HOME to find Andrew charging around after the dogs in the backyard, flapping his arms and yelling expletives. They scattered before him in waves like he was Moses parting the Red Sea. There was zero chance he'd be able to catch them. It would have been a comical scene except that I knew something pretty bad must have happened to get Andrew so riled up.

I hurried out the back door to investigate the scene of the crime, and to offer solace. "What'd they do this time?" I asked.

Andrew stooped down to pick up something tattered and torn. "This!" he said. He shook whatever it was, as though I would instantly say, *Oh no! Not that! Oh dear.* Except I still had no idea what it was.

The dogs had circled back to congregate behind my legs. I sat down on the deck, pulled them both onto my lap, and scratched their heads. Knowing they never had anything to fear from Andrew, they didn't run off as he came near this time.

Wearily, he sat on the deck beside me. "This," he repeated again, as he tossed the slobbered and chewed remains at me.

Then I actually did say, "Oh no. Not that. Oh dear." I looked over at him and could see this had really blown him out. "Your wallet. I'm really sorry."

Luckily, he'd been able to retrieve most of the contents undamaged, except for a few bills that looked as if they'd been through the wash one too many times. But Andrew found small consolation in the recovered goods. He'd been waging an internal war with himself over the dogs ever since they'd entered this second teething stage, and moments like these only fanned the flames. He really wanted to be a good sport, but he couldn't find enough about the dogs he considered endearing to offset what he found so aggravating. He hated how all this made him feel, because he really did want to find a way to let these dogs into his heart.

Andrew hadn't grown up in the company of a dog, and so never had the experience of being changed by one's love. Until Kiera-1. He did have moments where he was able to let her in and be touched by her. But it was a little too little, too late. Mostly, he'd spent those years being mildly annoyed at how much energy he thought I directed her way. Then he'd had something of a wake-up call after she died. He was devastated that he didn't fully realize how much he did love and appreciate her until after she was gone. He swore he wouldn't make that mistake a second time. He was going to get this dog "thing" if it killed him. He saw what they did for me, and hoped that someday he would be the beneficiary of those same feelings. But today wasn't going to be the day.

"This is really getting out of hand," he said. "I've lost count of how many shoes they've chewed. And now this! Nothing is safe."

"I know all this is really upsetting to you," I acknowledged. "But they'll be out of this teething stage in a few months. You just have to hang on until then, and then things will get sane again."

"Can't you at least teach them to leave the shoes alone?" Andrew implored.

It was a reasonable request, and I was doing my best to train the puppies. In fact, I was beginning to feel that all I was doing was training the puppies. In the meantime, I'd tried to train Andrew to get into the habit of putting any shoes not on his feet up and out of dog reach. He didn't consider this a practical solution, so I was elected the shoe police until the dogs finally lost interest in leather.

And gained interest in gopher holes. Gopher holes started appearing all over the yard. Except we didn't have any gophers. Magic just liked to dig up moles, voles, insects, and anything else that moved underground. And Kiera liked to sniff at whatever Magic unearthed. After clunking down into several of these potholes while mowing the lawn, Andrew would come in agitated.

"So this is all worth it to you?" came the oft-asked question.

No explanation I'd previously given seemed to satisfy him, so I would just nod unequivocally that it was. I knew Andrew was hoping for a more compelling answer, something that would help him understand what made it so worth it for me, while it was so clearly not worth it for him. It wasn't that I didn't find some of the things the dogs did annoying; it was just that I didn't see those things as defining characteristics of the dogs. Those were just stages they were growing through, not all that different from some toddler stages. Like the stage Cait went through when she was two, when she felt duty-bound to empty out every cupboard in the kitchen every chance she got.

What defined the dogs for me was the extraordinary company they provided, and the pleasure I'd get from petting them and watching them in the pure joy of play, chasing in wild circles, leaping and dodging and wheeling back for more. What defined the dogs for me was the love they gave me, a love that I never had to worry about going away or somehow not being enough.

I wanted to help Andrew get what it was the dogs did for me, I really did. I really hoped someday he might be able to start feeling it for himself. And I hated that it caused this rare tension between us.

The day the dogs chewed up his wallet, I remember Andrew asked me still again if I really thought it all worth it, and I had tried hard to help him understand.

I could feel myself starting to get defensive and I knew that wouldn't help the situation. I took a deep breath and decided instead to look at his repeated inquiries as indication of his genuine desire to understand.

"I don't know if I can ever explain this well enough for you," I said. "You know that my dogs have always played an important role in my life. I can count on them every day to make me laugh. As soon as I lay my eyes on them in the morning, or after I haven't seen them for a while, they just make me happy. When they're playing with each other, they are completely joyful. They're so entirely in the moment. They aren't wishing they were doing something else, or thinking about what else might be more fun. It makes me happy to witness that."

I searched Andrew's eyes hoping to find some flicker of understanding. I knew he intellectually understood it all, but this kind of understanding had proved of little use to him.

I continued, "And when I'm with them they are completely happy to be with me. Their feelings are always right on the surface for anyone to see. There's nothing to question or wonder about. They are who they are, without guile. It's not like being with people who judge you by what you say, or how you look, or what you do. I don't have to consider any of that nonsense, or whether I can really be who I am. I'm just with them. They're with me. None of us can imagine anything better. The thought just doesn't come into our heads."

I again looked for some kind of recognition.

Andrew smiled. "You know, sometimes I can't help thinking, the way you talk about those dogs, that you love them more than you love me."

I knew this was Andrew's joking way of saying his agitation had run its course, and he was ready to let the subject drop.

But I had detected an undertone in his voice that I didn't want to let slide.

"You're wrong," I said. "It's not more. It's different. There's a different affinity—"

Andrew interrupted me, "As far as I'm concerned, it's a bogus comment on my part."

Now he really had me. "Huh?" I sputtered.

"It's a bogus comment. All beings are worthy of the same love and attention. I've come to accept that, and I don't see anything wrong with it. I'm not judging you for loving your dogs. I just wish I could understand the depth of it. I wish its power would rub off on me."

I nodded.

"I don't want to be like this," Andrew continued as though carrying out an argument in his own head. "I want to love the dogs, because they're alive and part of my life, and because they don't ever stop extending love to me. It's not lost on me that they always run to greet me when I come in the door, tails wagging. I get that they never once seem anything other than beings put here to increase the general dosage of love and playfulness on the planet, and in our home.

"But it's a view I only seem able to hold when I'm not looking for a lost shoe, or not being woken up by barking in the middle of the night. I can't seem to do it when it's hard and inconvenient, when it means extending love for no other reason than extending it to another creature doing his or her best at what he or she feels the need to do."

He fell silent.

It bothered me that all of this was causing him such anguish. Especially when the only reason these dogs were in my life was because of a great act of unconditional love on his part. It seemed a cruel twist of fate. I didn't know what to do or say, so I didn't say anything.

He continued, "There's the concept of love, and then there's love. I know the difference. The difference plays itself out in my life day after day. The thing is, I don't know how a person makes himself more completely loving. I don't know how he learns to give without worrying about what he might get in return. I can do it with my children, a good deal of the time. I can do it with you, a good deal of the time. But what magic to be able to do it with strangers, or people you don't necessarily like, or dogs who eat your credit cards and spread your money to the winds. I want that magic. Who wouldn't want it?"

Indeed.

○

That night I fell asleep with dogs on my brain. I was thinking that it was true: My dogs were every bit as important to me as humans. And I gave them every consideration that I would Andrew or Cait. It wasn't hard for me to understand why Andrew might struggle with feeling that maybe my dog thing was a little much at times.

Not surprisingly, I felt as though I'd spent the whole night going from one dog dream to another—dreams that seemed so vividly real they blurred the lines between waking and sleeping. I awoke the next morning feeling subdued and pensive. The dreams, it seemed, had been trying to help me understand why I've had such a potent connection to, and concern for, my dogs.

The first dream had me cast in the life of an Eskimo, where my survival depended on my dogs. I was a man alone on a hunting expedition. I could only see one dog, but I knew I had more with me. The dog by my side was a Siberian Husky with copper coloring, and one blue eye and one brown. His job was to assist me in finding seal holes in the ice. He seemed to have an innate knack for doing this. He'd go out far ahead, tracking back and forth, until he'd spy an ice break and then let out a *Wooo woooo wooo*. Then he'd wait patiently by the hole until I arrived.

To help me retain body warmth, this Siberian of mine would curl up next to me, putting his nose under his tail, while I waited for a seal to come up to breathe. I became aware of how I kept shifting my eyes to his face for color contrast, to help prevent the glare from the snow from causing snow blindness during the long wait. It was a life of solitude in the extreme. From what I could see in the dream, this dog was my bastion of all things good. Because there was never a moment not spent together, eventually there was no need to speak. A minimal look or a hint of movement was enough to telegraph our thoughts to each other as loudly and clearly as words.

Then the setting in the dream began to shift. The images started flashing by, as if I were looking at one of those animation books where you flip the pages to make the pictures move. Life after life zipped past, each illustrating relationships with dogs that were of enormous importance to me. Then the pages slowed again, and settled onto a scene where I was a sheepherder in some bucolic, hilly region. Again, it was a life where I was alone with my dog (this time a black-and-white female Border Collie type) for days at a stretch. Even though this dog was a different breed and sex from the Husky, the sense was that they were one and the same dog, as though the spirit of this one in particular had been connected to me for lifetimes.

At those times when the sheep were back in the lower, enclosed fields, closer to home, and therefore in less danger, we'd spend our spare time entertaining each other. She had an incorrigible sense of humor. Her antics could keep me in stitches until I'd be out of breath and doubled over, laughing. Only then would she consider winding up with her grand finale. She'd round up the sheep into a tight bunch and then hop up and run across their backs as though on a runway, until, upon reaching the last back, she'd catapult herself into my arms, knocking me flat on the ground. Then she'd stand over me, licking the tears of laughter off my face. Not until this final escapade would she be capable of resting by my side, so I could pull the day's accumulation of burrs out of her fur.

As obedient and responsive as she was, there was also a piece of her that was essentially untamable; a wildness, a dogness that she kept for herself. She wasn't interested in trying to be human, as some dogs are. I'm sure this was because she wouldn't have considered it an improvement. She was wholly herself and not an extension of me. Though to watch us work was to watch perfected unity in motion—like watching a virtuoso violinist making child's play out of an intricate concerto: the strings representing the sheep, the flying bow my dog, and the flash of fingering my whistled commands. Our exquisite music reverberated across the hills daily.

Before my dreams were through, I dreamed about several more dogs who had played key roles with me. What all the vignettes had in common was a core dependency on a dog for my health and well-being. What was also made clear was how dogs played the role of savior: saving me from hunger; saving me from danger; saving me from loneliness; saving me from tasks I could not have accomplished alone.

If I was going to give credence to these dreams, it would appear that my instinctive relationship with my current dogs was not a new phenomenon, but rather something that was deeply, deeply embedded in my unconscious. I seemed predisposed to have an inborn allegiance with dogs that could easily be considered out of bounds to others.

If a Freudian was to interpret these dreams, he or she would have a field day talking about sublimation and displacement of intimacy issues, and projected animal desires, just for starters. (Though Freud himself, an avid Chow lover in his later years, might have allowed a broader view. He's been quoted as saying: "Dogs love their friends and bite their enemies, quite unlike people, who are incapable of pure love and always have to mix love and hate in their object-relations.")

On the other hand, a Buddhist might simply shrug and say, "Past life memories."

My take on it was more straightforward. I believed the dreams were speaking to the depth of my awareness of a sense of interrelationship with my dogs, where each party derived an acute sense of well-being, rightness, and safety from being together in what sometimes seemed an otherwise impossibly difficult world.

The other piece from those dreams that came through loud and clear was my attraction to working dogs.

To me, there were dogs, and then there were Dogs. Dogs with a lowercase *d* would include all the toy breeds and would fall into a category more akin to stuffed animals or dolls. Sweet, cuddly, fun to play with, but they didn't seem real to me. Not dogs I'd feel I could really count on in a pinch.

Then there were the play pals. These would include some of the sporting dogs. Fun to go out and run through the fields with, sometimes slightly goofy and gregarious, always good company (as all dogs are), but more apt than not to lick an intruder entering your house.

Then there were the capital *D* dogs. Dogs who weren't happy unless they had to use their brains and were given some kind of serious work to do—like guard, or herd, or anticipate your next move, or think for themselves.

This wasn't to say that I didn't truly appreciate all dogs, and wasn't happy for anyone who had one to love. And this was in no way to suggest that one type was better than another. Precisely, one of the great things about dogs is the wide selection from which each person can choose what suits his or her needs. It was just that what suited me was a working dog.

Statistics would point to the fact that since my first dog (a Sheltie) was a working dog, this would fairly reliably predict that my future dogs would also be working dogs. And while I think anyone who's had a dog would agree that, in most cases, our first dog does influence our future choices, I also believed there was something a little more complex at work governing my selections.

To the casual observer, I appear to be easygoing with hardly a care. But in actuality, I'm an intense person who lives an intense life. I try to be present and accounted for every day. What it comes down to for me is that I need a dog that I know will brave the elements, go through thick and thin, and walk to the ends of the earth with me. I need a dog who is as keyed in to me as I am to it. There's something very essential and primal about it for me. With my dogs, we're all on the same radar screen, responding to the same unseen forces at work, where instinct is often more trustworthy than reason.

And what I had in spades was two working dogs, who, right now, were both poking their cold noses under my arm, trying to rouse me out of bed to let them out. For this pack of three, it was time to start another day.

CHAPTER 11

The Coyotes Come

I WAS DREAMING that somewhere off in the distance dogs were barking frantically at a danger that had arrived silently during the night. I was so disturbed by this presence of something threatening, I awoke. I had to sit up to shake myself out of the dream, because I was still hearing frenetic barking. It took another second for me to register that it was my dogs barking, and they were outside toward the back of the property. I must have forgotten to close the dog door before going to bed.

A shiver of fear shot through me. This was not the normal, on-the-heels-of-a-squirrel barking. I scrambled out of bed and flung open our French doors. I stood peering out from the deck to see if I could detect what was going on. With the help of a late-summer, moonlit sky, I could see exactly what the commotion was about. My stomach knotted.

Kiera and Magic had somehow managed to get through our fence and were caught face-to-face in a Mexican standoff with one very large coyote.

I flew down the stairs and out the back door in nothing more than pajamas and bare feet, my heart beating as fast as hummingbirds' wings. Neighbors had alerted me that some coyotes had been charged in connection with the disappearance of a few cats in our neighborhood, and wouldn't be above nailing a small dog. Kiera was probably big enough to hold her own, but even though Magic had filled out some, I worried that he was still scrawny and small enough to be a potential target. In mid-stride, I grabbed a long stick from the ground that had fallen from one of our locust trees, and kept running.

At the back of our property there was a little land bridge that connected a small pond on one side and some brushy swamp on the other, with a tangle of dense thickets behind. As I closed the gap between my dogs and me, I could see that Magic had managed to corner the coyote back there, with Kiera a couple of feet behind for backup. They were lunging and barking ferociously while the coyote stood his ground, staring the two of them down. It appeared he was calmly considering his very limited options. I could hear a pack of coyotes not much further back in the brush signaling to him.

I called out to Magic and Kiera, stupidly thinking maybe they'd come. Magic stole a split-second look, which was all the coyote needed to turn tail and run. To my horror, Magic took off right after him, close on his heels. I screamed for him to come back and started sprinting after him. Kiera looked at me as if not sure what to do: Should she come to me, or should she go help Magic? Again, I heard the yipping and yelping of the pack. And then, sickeningly, I heard Magic stop barking. That made Kiera's decision for her. In a flash, she was out of sight, off to help Magic.

If the coyotes had set a trap for Magic, Kiera was running straight for it now. I took off after Kiera, screaming for them both to come back, but I was quickly stopped by impenetrable prickers and brush.

By this time, Andrew, fully dressed, had reached my side. He'd been awoken by my screams and had come racing out in time to capture the full picture. I looked at him in a state of total panic. I worried that Magic was a goner and was now afraid for Kiera.

We both searched again for a way to get through the tangle of thickets, with the same result: There was no way we could get through. The layout of our property was such that the back five acres ran parallel to the road we lived on. It would be quicker and easier to get where we needed to go by driving down the road and heading back in from a logging trail at the other end. Andrew told me to stand there and keep calling while he got into the car and tried to reach them from the back end.

He sped down the road and I kept calling. I'd stop every minute or so to listen. The woods were deathly silent. I trotted back and forth along the back edge searching, trying to bore through the dark shadows in an effort to get a glimpse of anything moving. I kept calling.

I don't know how long I was out there pacing before I saw Andrew's headlights coming back down the road. I held my breath in anticipation as he pulled in the driveway. I prayed that I'd see two dogs bound out when he opened the door. He exited the car alone. It felt as though a huge boulder had been dropped on my chest. Breathing required a massive effort. I was cursing myself for not having shut the dog door. Walking toward me, Andrew asked if the dogs had come back. Finding no extra air in my lungs with which to speak, I just shook my head no.

I found it ironic and irritating that at this particular moment I seemed to be caught in a sustained state of being fully present — a state that I'd been striving for through meditative practices for a long time, and could usually only maintain for brief periods. It was one of those moments where time got stuck and I was trapped in the Now, with all my senses painfully wedged open. All at once, I became aware of the cacophonous song of cicadas and bullfrogs tuning up like a noisy orchestra. I could hear every delicate birdcall, and catch every leaf faintly tinkle with the slightest breeze. I could feel the damp grass tickle under every footstep and feel the rays of the sunrise just peaking up over the horizon reaching out to touch my skin. Each Now folded into another Now, and another. Yet I wished I were anywhere else but in the Now. I wished I were back in bed sleeping through a bad dream. I wished I were wherever Kiera and Magic were, with my arms safely around them. I wished . . .

Just then, a black blur darted past my legs from behind and wheeled back around. This time, my scream was one of joy. It was Magic. He was in one piece, cheerfully wagging his tail as though he'd just sauntered back from a casual stroll. I pounced on him and squished him close to me, covering him with kisses. Then it dawned on me that if Magic had made it back, Kiera was probably all right, too. I sprang to my feet and urgently clapped my hands, calling for her. I wanted to get her back to me as fast as I could. Seconds later, she nonchalantly emerged from the thickets.

Andrew, taking advantage of our happy reunion, rounded us all up and shepherded us safely back into the house. He looked at the kitchen clock and then, with a raised eyebrow, at me. It was 5:30 A.M. We'd been launched into the day much too early.

While Andrew went back upstairs, hoping to get a little more sleep before the workday started, I couldn't have been more awake if I'd drunk a whole pot of espresso coffee. So I decided to do some research. With both dogs snuggled at my feet, I fired up the computer.

We'd been living with these coyotes encircling our lives for a while now. It was time to dig past the rumors, stereotypes, and romanticizing, and find out exactly what we were dealing with. I needed to know what kind of danger Magic and Kiera were really in. Had Kiera's and Magic's safe return been a lucky break, or should it have been expected? Did this mean I could not leave them out ever again, unless I was home and outside with them? Was Cait in any danger when she was swinging on her swings back by the garden? I needed to know.

Here's what I found:

Canis latrans (barking dog) is a relative of the wolf and domestic dog. Coyotes were originally native to the open plains of the West, but after the Gray Wolf (their main predator) was nearly exterminated, they were, for all intents and purposes, given a free pass to expand across the entire North American continent. They've inhabited New York State for about seventy years, with numbers estimated between fifteen and thirty thousand. They're thought to be most densely populated in the Adirondacks, for which I can vouch. Eastern Coyote males can grow to more than sixty pounds, although the majority weighs between thirty and fifty-five.

It's thought that most coyotes mate for life. They reach maturity by the age of two and from then on give birth to an annual litter of between two and ten pups. Only 5 to 20 percent of coyote pups survive their first year. Of those remaining, more than half will die before adulthood, mostly from human trapping, hunting, and poisoning. Those that do survive can live to be twelve years old.

Since coyotes are opportunistic eaters, they'll eat whatever they can find, including vegetation and fruit. Primarily nocturnal, they hunt from dusk until dawn — unless food is scarce, in which case they'll hunt day and night. Because they don't share the intricate pack hierarchy (and therefore lack the extensive cooperative hunting skills) of wolves, they're not as likely to bring down large prey such as deer or large livestock. If caught feeding on such an animal, the coyote has more than likely just had the good fortune of finding one already dead.

New York coyotes survive on rabbits, woodchucks, mice, and a small proportion of deer (mostly scavenged), along with a variety of fruits and vegetables found left in fields. While specific coyotes can pose a real problem to specific livestock, overall, according to environmentalists and biologists, the species' reputation for killing livestock has been blown out of proportion.

It's believed that coyotes as a whole are not necessarily harmful, because so much of their diet consists of destructive rodents. In the Northeast, uncontrolled domestic dogs are a much greater threat, responsible for losses to livestock far exceeding losses from coyotes.

Normally, coyotes pose no danger to adults, but I did find that there are potential risks to pets and small children. Of course, there can never be any guarantee or prediction of safety from any form of wildlife, particularly if the animals are cornered, sick, or protecting young or territory. But coyotes are by nature fearful of humans. While attacks on small pets do occur, attacks on people are still extremely rare. In all known cases the coyote had lost its fear of humans because people were feeding the animals.

The ASPCA (American Society for the Prevention of Cruelty to Animals) had these suggestions for warding off and avoiding encounters with coyotes:

First, they're quick to remind people that a coyote that hasn't been habituated to humans is naturally timid and, if healthy, very unlikely to approach. It's much more likely that you'd be spotted and avoided by a coyote long before you'd see it. Chances are that if you ever do see a coyote, it will be from a distance.

That said, the first suggestion is not to leave small children or small pets (especially cats) unattended. Avoid putting pets out alone from dusk to dawn when coyotes are more likely to be active. High fences are recommended.

Second, don't feed coyotes. This may seem obvious, but you could be contributing food unknowingly, such as left-out pet food, garbage, dropped fruit from trees, and vegetable gardens. Even bird feeders can become a source of food in a harsh winter.

The ASPCA had this to say if you do come face-to-face with a coyote: Don't turn your back or run. Act aggressively toward it. Yell, throw your arms up, kick your legs (nearly the opposite of what you'd do in a situation with an aggressive dog). If you can find anything handy to arm yourself with, like a stick, do so.

○

I'd learned what I needed to know. I got a children's book on coyotes out of the library to read to Cait. This gave me an opportunity to talk with her. She was excited to think that we had some living right nearby. She thought they were cute and wanted to know why we couldn't capture one as a pet. I explained that wild animals really only did well when they were allowed to be wild. It wouldn't be fair to them, or safe for us, to keep one as a pet.

She asked if she saw one, could she go over and pet it. That gave me the opening I was looking for to instruct her, without scaring her, on what to do if she ever encountered one. To make sure that she really understood, we went outside where I had her play-act what she would do if one came into the backyard. She banished the imaginary coyotes with a flourish.

As for Magic and Kiera, I took that morning's escapades as a valuable forewarning. I would not be so careless again; I'd make sure the dog door was closed at night. And, in general, I'd keep a watchful eye out.

The sense I had after completing my research was that coyotes are here to stay. Despite aggressive efforts to exterminate these animals, they continue to survive and thrive. Biologists and environmentalists say that coyotes are necessary to preserve the balance of nature, and suggest that it's to our advantage to learn to live with them around farms and fringe areas as resident rodent controls.

While I would recognize and deal with the potential threat to my dogs and daughter, I came away feeling respect and admiration for their tenacity, intelligence, and adaptability, and wonder at their curiosity and playfulness.

CHAPTER 12

Mud Slide

LOOKING BACK, THE signs had been piling up. Magic had been leaving a trail of clues for months. They surfaced slowly at first, making it easy to overlook them—that was until the dam broke and caught us all in a mud slide, sweeping us away by forces beyond our control.

I looked at the clock as the phone rang. It was too early in the morning to be good news. Magic, who'd been sleeping under my arm, accidentally slipped off the bed as I reached over to grab the receiver. He jumped back up, licked my face, and rearranged himself on my feet. Kiera preferred sleeping in front of the glass doors, absorbing the cold January air before it could creep into the room. The call was from Andrew. After he apologized for waking me up, there was a long silence. It was a silence that spoke volumes; a silence that told me Andrew's father had died sometime during the night.

I made arrangements for my mother to watch Cait and the dogs, and made the drive to Rhode Island. Andrew, with his brothers and sister, had been at Joe's bedside, holding vigil for the past week. The cancer raging through Joe's body had finally taken him.

By the time I got there, Andrew had collected himself and was faring better than I'd expected. He'd worked very hard for the last decade to create the kind of relationship with his father that he'd always wanted, and he felt that he'd succeeded. There'd been nothing left unsaid.

At the wake, I watched Andrew greet the long line of people who streamed through: shaking hands, hugging, engaging them in talk, nodding as he listened, smiling, laughing, crying. It was doing him good to hear all these people who also loved Joe come and tell their stories about him.

I loved Joe, and always felt lucky to have him for my father-in-law. But my tears were as much for my own father who had died just a few years before. If it was possible, I'd found myself missing my dad more and more with each passing day, and this déjà vu wasn't helping any to soothe the ache, though it did help me begin to identify what the source of that ache was.

My father had been the one who'd taught me all of the skills I'd need to go out into the world, to take care of myself. He didn't care that I was a girl; he felt my sister and I should know how to do everything his sons knew how to do. He spent a lot of time teaching me anything he could think of that would offer me self-sufficiency and freedom. He taught me how to think for myself. He taught me how to drive a car. He taught me how to use carpenter tools as well as any carpenter. He taught me how to run a business. And what he couldn't teach me, he taught me where to go to find the answers.

I'm sure that by the time he died, he thought he'd taught me every important thing there was to know in order for me to live a successful and happy life. And I'd have to agree—except for one crucial piece—he never taught me how I could learn to live without him.

○

Back home, Andrew seemed to fall into a state of calm composure. I knew the fallout would seep out in the days and months ahead. I knew Andrew would have his hands full for a while just getting up and out of bed each day.

My mother stayed an extra day so I could get caught back up at work without having to worry about Cait. I came home to a freshly cleaned house and dinner on the table. The dogs hovered by gently nudging and licking Andrew, to remind him, it seemed, that his life was still full of love. And Cait took to waiting on her dad while he watched TV, getting him snacks. Then she'd sit right up close to him on the couch, serving as a flying buttress, making sure there was no chance he could sink or topple over.

I felt sad for all of us. I knew what an important role Joe had served for Andrew and what a hole his death would leave. And Cait had had to deal with more death in her young life than most people do by their twenties and thirties. (She'd faced three losses on Andrew's side, and seven on mine.) At first, this had made her afraid to let me out of her sight, because she thought I might unexpectedly "fly up to Heaven," too. This turned into a fear that besieged her to the point of incapacitation. It got so bad that I had to take her out of preschool that first year and keep her with me until she could regain her sense of balance and trust in the world. During that time, we did a lot of talking about life and death. She'd finally come to acquire the view, much like someone living on a farm, that death was just a natural part of life. We'd taken it another step, and she was able to accept that by no means was it the end of our ability to stay in touch with those who'd passed on.

Whenever she'd notice Andrew feeling sad, she'd remind him, "Daddy, just think of Beepa like he's in the next room. Even though we can't see him, we can still talk to him through the door. And he can still hear us." Andrew, knowing she was saying this as much to reassure herself as him, would smile, nod, and give her a big hug. Then Cait would come to me later and whisper, "Mommy, I feel so sad for Daddy because he's an orphan now."

In her mind, she couldn't imagine any love more powerful than the love for her mother and father. Equally, she couldn't imagine any loss more devastating. She and I would redouble our efforts to keep Andrew cheered up.

○

Before my mother left the next morning, she asked if there was something wrong with Magic. I wasn't aware of anything, so I asked her if there had been a problem.

She told me that Magic had had a few unprovoked aggressive encounters with her German Shepherd, Asia. She said they happened out of nowhere and were over just as fast, but it had upset her. Asia was getting old, and my mother was understandably very protective of her. I told her I'd keep an eye on Magic, and work with him more around other dogs. That seemed to satisfy her. We hugged, I thanked my mother, and she started back for home.

I thought about what my mother had said after she left. It struck me as odd that Magic would go after Asia. When I had first introduced them to each other, I thought Magic might feel jealous because Kiera adored Asia, so I kept an eagle eye, ready to anticipate anything. But Magic was genuinely gaga over Asia, too. All three had played beautifully together then and since.

Then there was the not minor detail that Asia was about the size of a small pony; she seriously outweighed and towered over Magic. Magic could be a pest—he still had a lot of puppy energy at a year and a half old—but he wasn't stupid. I decided that what probably happened was that Asia must have bumped into Magic a little too hard while they were playing, and Magic got hurt. He'd momentarily gone after Asia to let her know that she was being too rough. That had to have been it. Mystery solved to my satisfaction, I put the incident out of my head.

A few months passed, and the warmer weather helped to raise everyone's spirits. Cheryl asked me to go with her to an obedience show one weekend. It would be a lighthearted change of scenery. Cait assumed she was invited; she considered Cheryl her friend, too. And it was Magic's turn for an outing, so we three took off.

I wasn't surprised to find Cheryl waiting for us with a new rescue dog in tow. I gave her a big hug and knelt down to pet this new Aussie mix, who was a little shy but very gentle. Then I went around to put Magic on his leash and let him out of the car. Happy to be sprung, he went right over to greet Cheryl. Then, for no apparent reason, he turned and snapped at the rescue dog. I was able to maneuver him away before he could make contact.

Flustered, I immediately apologized to Cheryl. Nonplussed, she suggested we try working with Magic to see if we could get him to relax and behave with her dog. We tried several approaches and click/treats for calm behavior. Magic seemed to get how he was supposed to behave. But as soon as we started to walk over to the ring, Magic went for the dog again. Cheryl scooted the dog to her other side for safety. Then she just shrugged and said, "Like people, sometimes dogs just don't like each other." Chagrinned, I smiled, and nodded, and put some distance between Cheryl's dog and mine. To my relief, Magic was his lovable, cuddly, mild-mannered self for the rest of the afternoon.

McLean, my stepson, usually spent half the week with us. That night, when he got home for dinner, the dogs ran out to greet him as usual. McLean tussled with them both as usual. He walked through the kitchen door, holding it open for Kiera and Magic to run through before he slid it closed. Then, bizarrely, as McLean turned around to sit down, I watched Magic jump up and nip him in the seat of his pants. Magic had never put a tooth on anyone before, even playing. He'd only gotten a mouthful of blue jeans for his trouble, but McLean whirled around in total surprise. Magic quickly pulled away in retreat and then went back up to McLean with tail wagging, looking for more pets. McLean, sure this must have been a playful act on Magic's part, started tussling with him some more. Magic seemed to enjoy the play as he always had. Still, I suggested to McLean that it might be better if, when he played with Magic, he didn't get him so excited.

These few occurrences weren't enough to set off any alarms in my head. Cheryl had mentioned that male dogs (even neutered ones like Magic) were getting their adult hormones at around a year and a half to two years old, and he was probably just starting to feel his oats. I figured that must be what it was — Magic had simply hit his bratty teenage phase. The rest of that spring and summer passed quietly.

○

Fall rolled around and Cait was happy to be back in school, which allowed me to put in longer days at the office. The days were flying by. I'm not sure Kiera and Magic would have agreed. They were spending considerably more time alone.

It wasn't long before I noticed that Magic and Kiera had taken to chasing after anyone on foot or bike. Magic would tear from one end of the property to the other in a heated sprint, and then race back again, barking furiously the whole time. Kiera would follow in reluctant pursuit. I wasn't happy with this behavior, but they were safely behind our fence, far from the road. And I rationalized it by thinking at least they were getting a lot of aerobic exercise. It didn't register as something I should have stopped, or as another change in Magic's behavior.

When Magic started routinely trying to nip McLean anytime he turned his back, a hairline crack started opening in my denial. My first prescription was to have McLean stop all roughhousing with Magic immediately and permanently. (I need to explain on McLean's behalf that the roughhousing I'm talking

about was usually tug-of-war or something else seemingly in-
nocuous—which Magic typically initiated.) Then I asked him if
he would help me work with Magic to see if we could redirect
this behavior. An avowed dog lover, he agreed. There wasn't
anything McLean wouldn't do for Magic, or Kiera for that matter. I dug out my clicker and we got started.

I made sure that anytime McLean was coming, I had Magic
on a leash waiting. When McLean would get to the door, I'd put
Magic in a sit; McLean would enter and give Magic a treat.
Then he would calmly go and sit down. Magic wouldn't be allowed to go over to him until he was sitting. This seemed to
break up the frenetic greeting cycle that had developed. When it
was time for McLean to leave, I'd again have Magic on a leash.
McLean would gently pet him, and back out of the house while
I kept Magic in a sit.

While this managed the problem, it didn't correct it. Anytime
I'd try to progress Magic to the next step toward getting him off-
leash again, he'd revert right back to trying to nip McLean.

After several weeks, I was starting to get discouraged. In the
midst of all this, there had been other worrisome little signs crop-
ping up. But it wasn't until Cait had a little friend over to play that
I had my first real sense that things might be getting out of hand.

When we got home with Cait's friend, I explained about our
greeting routine. I'd put Magic on a leash. Cait and her friend
would sit at the kitchen table armed with treats. With her permission, after explaining what to expect, I let Magic go over
(still on leash) so she could drop treats for him on the floor.
Magic sniffed, ate his treats, and then I let him outside to play
with Kiera, as I always did. I closed the dog door so the girls
could play freely inside.

After playing in Cait's room for a while, the two girls came
back into the kitchen for a snack. When Magic saw Cait's friend
through the glass, he exploded at the door—lunging, snarling,

and scratching to get in. Kiera looked at Magic, not knowing what to do. She barked a couple of times for good measure, thinking maybe Magic knew something she didn't know, and she should get in on the act just in case. I made light of it to the little girl, so she wouldn't be afraid, but I was very disturbed by what I was seeing. This wasn't normal. This wasn't my sweet Magic. It was as if something else had possessed him.

A little voice in the back of my head said, *Houston, we have a problem*.

I sent the girls upstairs and called a carpenter friend of mine. "Jason, I need you to come over as soon as you can fit me in. I need you to put in a stockade fence with no gates that I can put the dogs into through a second dog door from the pantry."

Not used to such an abrupt start to our conversations (Jason and I had been friends for years), he asked, "What's up?"

I couldn't bring myself to say that I thought I had another aggression problem on my hands, so I just said, "I need someplace I can keep the dogs when Cait has friends over. You know how well herding dogs and flapping, high-pitched, squealing little kids go together."

"Yeah, draws 'em like flies to doodoo . . ." Jason had his own experiences with herding dogs.

We both laughed, and he promised to get over as soon as he could. Before we hung up, I emphasized again that I needed this done ASAP. Then I went to dig out a box from the attic that I'd hoped I'd never have to see again. It contained all my books on dog aggression. I started rereading.

My plan was to limit as best I could exposing Magic to the situations that seemed to trigger this aggression. That meant no spur-of-the-moment friends over for Cait, no playing with McLean, and no unexpected company. If someone had to come over, Magic would be closed off with Kiera up in my bedroom for the duration.

Cait asked why she couldn't have friends come unless it was planned and Magic was crated. I explained that it wouldn't be forever, just until I could make sure having people over again was safe. Cait, not really understanding the problem said, "Mom, I would never let anybody hurt Magic." In Cait's mind, Magic could do no wrong.

I called Jason again after a few days to bug him about getting that fence up. He told me he wouldn't be able to get over with samples or to measure for another few weeks. I let go of all pretenses; keeping Magic safe from himself and everybody else was paramount for me now. I told Jason I didn't care what the damn fence looked like; I just wanted it up as quickly as possible. I eyeballed the dimensions of the side yard and told him how many sections he needed to get. He promised to get right on it.

A few weeks into our self-imposed exile, Magic was still getting easily keyed up. While Magic was always nothing but gentle and loving to Andrew, me, and Cait, he'd reached the point where I knew I couldn't trust him with anyone else. He'd become totally unpredictable. I couldn't tell whether he would lick or try to bite until it was too late. I think it was because he didn't know what he was going to do, either. It was as though something else had taken over that he couldn't control. I could see this weird confusion hitting him, and still nothing I tried with training was having any effect.

○

I was waiting at home for a repairman to show up to fix my stove. Since the office manager wouldn't narrow down a time as to when this person might arrive, I'd asked that he call before he came. A few hours later, he showed up at the front door unannounced. He introduced himself as Terry, and asked to be shown to the stove. Magic and Kiera were outside in the back playing, so rather than walk Magic past this man to get him upstairs, which would cause everyone avoidable agitation, I just closed the dog door and left them outside. Terry went to work and I went back into the study to write.

I heard the dogs barking. They'd discovered the strange truck in our driveway. As long as they weren't clawing at the kitchen door . . . Then I heard high-pitched whining and scratching at the mudroom door. I shuddered with the awareness of what that sound meant. I leapt up and raced to the door to lock it. Before I could reach it, Kiera had opened it and Magic, sounding like Cujo, flew past me and darted around the hall into the kitchen. Kiera wasn't far behind.

I yelled for Terry to get up on the counter, as I vaulted over our couch trying to shave a second off my time to get to them as fast as I could. Terry didn't stand a chance; Magic was on him before he had time to turn around. In the three seconds it took me to get from the living room to the kitchen, I knew Magic had already landed two good bites, because they'd corresponded with two very loud yelps of human pain followed by a string of profanities.

I ran in, caught Magic, and dragged him away by the collar. I got him and Kiera outside again—all doors locked this time— and went back to check on Terry. He alternated between rubbing his thigh and calf while cursing nonstop. All I could do was stand there wringing my hands and apologizing like a broken record. I explained that I was an EMT, and asked if he wanted me to take a look. He said no, he was all right. He said he'd been bitten a bunch of times—hazard of the job and all—and that he just wanted to go home. I breathed a huge sigh of relief as I closed the door behind him.

Magic and Kiera stood barking until he was out of the driveway, and then they came trotting over to the kitchen door, tails wagging, as though it was just any other day. I went outside and sat on the grass so they could climb all over me. I finally caught their wiggling bodies and hugged onto them.

They both immediately rolled onto their backs for tummy rubs. Kiera became absorbed by a dragonfly that had landed on her and decided to go chase it.

I hugged onto Magic. "Hey, my boy," I whispered, "what's gotten into you; what demons are you fighting?" I held his slender face nestled between my hands, and kissed his nose. He pressed his skinny little body against mine and licked away my tears.

That night, I picked up yet another book on the causes and treatment of aggression. The first paragraph stated that one of the first steps in evaluating an aggression problem was to get the dog checked by a vet to make sure there was no underlying health problem causing the behavior change. If any of the other books I'd read had made this suggestion, it hadn't registered. But this time it leapt off the page at me. Maybe there was something physically wrong with Magic. That's the only thing that would make sense. I called the vet and made an appointment.

Magic was a licker, especially when he was nervous. Dr. Cris leaned his face in to make it easier for Magic to give as many licks as he wanted, while he continuously petted and stroked and talked to Magic in a reassuring voice. He listened to my concerns; I explained what I'd been observing and concluded that, in general, Magic had become more frenzied and not himself.

Magic's physical turned up nothing unusual. The next step was blood tests. A few days later, Dr. Cris called with the results. Magic had Lyme disease. He needed to be put on antibiotics.

As soon as I hung up from the call, I went to research the effects and progression of Lyme in dogs. I found that it could affect neurological functioning and did sometimes manifest as an aggression disorder. But I also couldn't rule out Magic's early abuse coming back to haunt him, causing him to behave more aggressively now that he was hormonally mature enough to act with more confidence. I wouldn't be able to tease it apart until Magic had been on antibiotics for a while, until the Lyme was under control.

I knew I had to go into serious management mode. If there was a neurological problem, that meant Magic would have little or no control over these "episodes." That had surely seemed the case with his attack on Terry.

It was time to step up the rehabilitation program. Having converted to clicker training, I wanted to find a local clicker trainer who also specialized in aggression. My search turned up nothing. That night I logged on to my favorite dog training site: ClickerSolutions. I'd remembered reading some posts by a clicker trainer, Bob Bellamy, who was known for his work with aggressive dogs. I'd read accounts of some amazing turnarounds he'd had with severely aggressive dogs and figured if anybody could help me, maybe he could. I e-mailed him, explained what had happened, and asked if I could talk with him by phone (he was located on the West Coast). He agreed to a phone consultation later that evening.

I called at the appointed time. Bob asked me about Magic's background, and what I saw as the progression of events. I filled him in, starting with what I knew about Magic's days as a puppy before he came to us.

"The first thing I have to tell you," Bob said, "is there are no guarantees with any of this. It's going to be a long-term project that will have its ups and downs. Even if you have some success, this is almost certain to be a lifelong issue. Training away from behaviors isn't going to be easy—"

I interrupted him, "Bob, I love this dog. I'm ready to do whatever it takes. As the saying goes, the journey of a thousand miles begins with one step."

"That's exactly the attitude you're going to need, Karen," he answered. "Okay, let's get started."

We spent the next two hours with Bob outlining a step-by-step program, while I took copious notes.

○

I began Magic's rehabilitation in earnest. I started coming home early from work, before Cait would get home from school, so I could get in a few sessions of training each day. And I had a pile of recommended reading on my nightstand that I'd plow through each night, highlighting and taking notes as I read. I'd go as far as I could until I'd get stuck or confused and then I'd call or e-mail Bob and go over whatever part of the program was giving me trouble. One of the first things Bob stressed was to manage those triggers that I wasn't able to work with. Under no circumstances was Magic to be allowed to self-reinforce any of the aggressive behaviors he'd developed. If I wasn't in a position to work with Magic when something came up, I should keep him closed off in another room. The point wasn't to keep Magic always off somewhere isolated, which could create other problems, but rather to make sure that if I wasn't in a position to deal with things, at least I wouldn't be putting myself or Magic into a bad situation. Bob explained that if there were inconsistencies here, Magic would take this to mean that sometimes his behavior was acceptable and sometimes it wasn't, and therefore it would always be worth a shot to see if he could get away with it.

The one part of clicker training that can be a challenge is to learn to click at just the right moment. Potentially, if you didn't click at the instant when the dog was doing exactly what you wanted, you might inadvertently wind up reinforcing something you didn't mean to. For instance, instead of reinforcing a proper sit, if you were off a second and the dog had just barked after it sat, you might be reinforcing the bark. When I first started training Kiera and Magic, I didn't worry if I was getting everything perfectly right. I wasn't going to get neurotic over whether every click perfectly matched every desired behavior. I knew I was accurate enough often enough that my dogs had no trouble figuring it out. My early days working with them had been relaxed, fun, and rewarding.

Not anymore. Overnight, it seemed, I'd turned into a total lunatic. There was so much riding on all of this; I felt I couldn't afford to make any mistakes. I went from feeling fairly confident with knowing what I was doing to feeling totally insecure and inept. Whereas I had no trouble before breaking down the criteria into small pieces, I was erratically lumping steps together here and there. The major difference was that I'd gone from training in a low-stress situation to trying to train in the midst of an aggressive outburst.

Magic would escalate so fast that I couldn't even see what the different elements were that went into the situation so I could break them apart to start working with them individually. I'd try to find a way to quickly end that training session on a positive note by getting Magic to do anything I could click and treat him for. Then I'd have to go sit down and try to figure out what had just happened and how I could better prepare for it the next time.

I'd e-mail Bob to report what happened, and he'd e-mail me back outlining what I'd done wrong and what I needed to do to better break down the criteria—coaching, correcting, and encouraging the whole time. I'd try that, report back, and so it'd go.

After an afternoon of this, I'd be completely wrung out. And there would be many afternoons like this. It went on for months. Sometimes after these sessions, I'd just grab Magic and Kiera and go play in the backyard. Magic would revert to my sweet boy who couldn't give me enough love or get close enough to snuggle with me. We'd play three-way Frisbee until we were all exhausted and then I'd lie on the grass and they'd pile on top of me.

Several months went by without any significant improvement. I'd been mostly concentrating on working with Magic using McLean and one friend of Cait's who wasn't afraid of Magic. This was mainly because, not surprisingly, it was hard to find willing volunteers to work with what appeared to be a vicious dog. So we just kept plugging away with what we had.

One interesting thing that did start happening was that Kiera started acting as Magic's guardian, as though he were one of her flock that she needed to protect and keep safe. When he'd tear after someone on a bike, she'd try to race ahead and get him turned back before he could reach the fence. And when he'd look as if he was going to jump and nip at McLean, she'd try to insert herself in between the two. It was as though she, too, knew something was wrong with Magic that he couldn't help, and she was trying her best to look after him.

A few months more passed with up-and-down progress, as Bob had predicted. And I kept up with my reading. I'd also spoken with a behaviorist. Magic's aggression had a label: It was a combination of fear aggression with a dose of territorial aggression thrown in. Because Magic's early history included fearful and unpleasant experiences, whenever he was confronted with something unfamiliar—and the key point here is that this only occurred on *his* property, *his* territory (thus the territorial aggression)—he would be likely to fight. The behaviorist went on to explain that the snarling attack was indicative of a dog who was strongly aggressive and only slightly fearful. The touch of fear was what turned the silent attack of a confident dog into the snarling attack of the conflicted dog. He added that this was not a dog I would ever be able to take for granted, because the impulse to attack would remain extremely strong.

I was living in a near-constant state of worry that some unexpected person would show up and make the mistake of thinking that this little runt of a barking dog couldn't possibly be a threat, wouldn't possibly do anything harmful. Knowing that I had a ticking time bomb on my hands, I got tired of waiting for Jason to get over. I went to a building supply store and ordered the stockade fence myself. It was going to be an effort to put it up, but the peace of mind it would give me and the safety it would buy for Magic would be worth the hard labor.

That night the coyotes must have made a kill right across the road in the clearing in front of our house. The rabid snarls, screams, and tearing sounds were terrible. In a matter of minutes, the night was silent once again. I went to sleep thinking that I was surrounded by wild dogs—inside and outside my house.

○

Several days later, I had to have another guy over to make some repairs on the house. But I was ready this time. I kept the dogs locked away with me in another room while the man worked. He arrived early in the morning, and I had Andrew let him in and get him set up with whatever he needed. He was to yell for me from where he was if he needed help, and I would come to him.

Initially, Magic seemed okay. I was working at my desk and both dogs were settled on my feet. But Magic must have heard something because he started pacing and barking. Then he went to the window and saw the truck in the driveway. I watched him transform into a different dog right before my eyes. His eyes glazed over and I couldn't even get him to respond to his name. Tragically, at that moment, without giving any warning, Andrew entered the room to tell me he was taking Cait to school and going into work.

Like a heat-seeking missile, Magic shot at Andrew, sinking his teeth deep into Andrew's hand. After Andrew screeched, Magic seemed to register who he'd bitten. He was still a screwed-up mess, but he didn't try to bite Andrew again. He started running around in nervous circles and whining as if to say, *I'm so sorry, I'm so sorry. I didn't mean to do that.* Andrew just stood there freaked out, looking at his hand in disbelief.

I had three nut cases on my hands—Andrew, Magic, and me—as I put a butterfly stitch on Andrew's palm. But if you'd been standing in the corner, you'd have only witnessed two. I forced myself into a detached mode, as though I'd just arrived at the scene of an accident, and I needed to quickly and efficiently tend to the victims.

Andrew kept repeating, "I can't believe he did that." Magic continued to circle. I calmly told Andrew to go to the doctor's after he dropped Cait off because he'd need a couple of stitches in order for the wound to heal properly. I knew his state of mind was in far worse shape than his hand. I knew he wanted me to say something to him to make it all right again, to make this all go away. I knew he wanted Magic to make it as badly as I did, and this moment of realizing that Magic had become a danger now to everyone except to me was as bad as it gets.

I also knew Andrew wanted to stay and talk it out. But I didn't want to talk. I just wanted him to leave. I just wanted to be alone with Magic. There was nothing to say. I knew what I had to do. I had been working intensively on this problem with Magic daily for over a year now. I had given it everything I had, and then some. What if it had been Cait who'd walked through that door? The bite level would have been at her face. There was no more "next thing" to try. There was no more "there" to get to. This was not a casual or impulsive decision; we'd played out the string. I adored this dog and my heart felt smashed into a million bits knowing what I had to do, but there was no other choice I could responsibly make.

○

The last hours I had with Magic I wanted to be happy hours. Just him and me and the love we shared. I put Magic in the car and drove to the park. We walked a ways, and then I sat down and just held him in my arms.

Dr. Cris met me in the hospital parking lot. (I didn't have him come to the house because I knew Magic would lose it again.) I was sitting in the backseat of my car with Magic in my lap when he came to the window. He asked me if I was sure this is what I wanted to do.

I wanted to scream, *No, this isn't what I want to do! This isn't what I want to have happen!* Instead, I answered, "Please, if you can tell me a way this doesn't have to happen, tell me. Is there some magic person I can take him to, some magic pill I can give him?"

Dr. Cris knew how far I'd gone to try to make this all work. He knew about the behaviorists and trainers and medications. He knew how much I loved this dog.

He quietly answered, "I don't know many people who would have done as much as you have."

I held Magic in my arms, whispering my love to him. I promised him that I would find a way to make his life count; I would not let this all be for nothing. The injection took hold and my little boy slipped away. I buried my face in his still-warm body and silently sobbed. It was all over. It was finally all over.

Dr. Cris asked if I was going to be okay, if I wanted him to stay with me for a while. I could feel a cold numbness to the outside world already start to set in. I thanked him and said no. I just needed a minute to collect myself and then I'd take my boy home.

○

When I got Magic home that day, I called Andrew at work to come and help me bury him by his favorite spot. Andrew screamed home in record time and leapt out of the car. He was devastated that this was the way it had turned out, and he blamed himself for what happened.

Later, he and I went for a short walk so we could talk without Cait overhearing our conversation. (I'd yet to figure out what I was going to tell her.)

I tried to explain to Andrew that I knew he would be incapable of making the decision I knew had to be made. I felt it would have been cruel to put him through that. And I secretly felt that Magic was my love, and my responsibility. Nobody knew him better than me. Nobody knew how hard I worked to change the outcome that Bob Bellamy had warned was probable. Nobody could possibly know what it took out of me to have Magic put down.

The next thing I knew, in the midst of our conversation, I was lying on the ground looking up at Andrew. I'd blacked out. My body had a habit of shutting down on me anytime my emotions got severely overloaded. Andrew hoisted me back up on my feet and we continued walking.

I knew Andrew was asking me to help him with his grief and sadness, and I was willing to. I knew I'd have to. I'd have to deal with him, with Cait, with Kiera. They would all need me.

We got back to the house and Cait met us at the door. "Mom, have you seen Magic? He didn't come to greet me when I got home from school. And he's not coming when I call him. Do you think something's happened? Do you think a coyote . . . ?"

On her own, Cait had noticed Magic's absence and at first assumed he was out playing somewhere in the yard. But he'd been missing long enough for her to feel troubled. I looked at her worried expression thinking, *One down, two to go.* We sat down and talked.

Andrew and I agreed that she should be shielded from the truth for fear that news of another death would precipitate another setback in her trust for life. I'd tell her at a time when we were a little further away from so many losses.

I told her, "You know how Magic was confused this morning and didn't know who Dad was; well, I've found a woman to take Magic to her home and help him get better."

Cait asked, "Can he come home soon?"

I said, "He probably won't be coming back home for a while. He needs a lot of help. But this is a really nice lady and she'll really love him."

Cait said, "Not as much as we do . . ."

"No, not as much as we do. But she'll love him a lot," I whispered, trying to hold back my tears.

Seeing that I was upset, too, Cait gave me a hug and patted my back. "I'm sad Magic won't be with us, Mom, but I'm happy he'll be getting help somewhere safe."

How I wished that were the truth.

And Kiera . . . Kiera spent that first night looking everywhere for Magic. She scoured every inch of our property, first inside and then out. (I'd closed her in our bedroom while we buried Magic because I'd only felt capable of dealing with one thing at a time.) She'd keep coming over to me with those questioning eyes, and place a paw in my lap as if it were an invitation to take her and show her where Magic was. As if she were saying, *Come on, let's go! We gotta find him. What are you waiting for?*

After Andrew and Cait fell asleep, I took Kiera outside to Magic's resting place, took off the slate covering I'd put over him to prevent the coyotes from digging him up, and called her over so she could smell the ground. "He's here, my love. I'm so sorry." She looked at me, looked at Magic's spot, sniffed and pawed at it and let out a lone howl. It was the first time I let myself really cry.

I'd spent so much of my life trying to control life's variables to keep those I loved protected and safe. It was as if life were saying to me, *The joke's on you! Life is uncontrollable. And love can't protect or keep safe.*

○

Not long after, having thought I'd spared Cait for a while, she announced to me that she knew Magic was dead. I asked her what made her think that. She told me that she'd just seen Magic come running through the dog door. And when she ran after him to find him, he wasn't there, and that meant he was dead.

Looking at Cait's face, there was certainty. She knew, so there was no point in lying. No matter how well intentioned I'd been in trying to protect her, she was going to have to face this loss. We cried together, and laughed a little too, remembering all the fun times and the things that we loved about Magic.

And then I fell into a cavernous funk that seemed unending. I knew I needed to release the grief but I was afraid that once I started I wouldn't be able to stop. Instead I took to replaying everything that had happened, trying to find a way that I could have made it turn out differently. I was haunted by these thoughts. What if I'd paid more attention to and acted on the signs earlier, maybe tried to find a specialized trainer nearby to have taken him and worked with him personally, no matter what the cost? And the *if onlys* could be brutal. Mostly, I'd just think about how much I loved Magic and how much I missed him.

The numbness that started at the vet's began to slowly creep through my veins. As the weeks passed, I could feel myself pulling farther into myself than I knew was healthy. It wasn't that I stopped loving Andrew, Cait, or Kiera. It was just that I stopped caring about anything. Nothing mattered to me one way or the other anymore.

After a few months of this, Andrew finally let me have it one night. "I know you've been going through a hard time, but you've got to snap yourself out of it. It's not fair to Cait and me. And Kiera's so worried about you, she won't let you out of her sight."

I reached down and stroked Kiera, who was on my feet. "It's not like I haven't been trying," I said.

"If I could bring Magic back for you, if I could take that day back, I would. But I can't. No one can. You just have to find a way to get past it—for all of us," Andrew said.

"I wish it was that simple," I said. "It's not just about Magic. It's not just about the journey he took me on. I think it's deeper; it has to do with something that I've been searching for that feels as though it's slipping through my fingers. I've been trying to figure out how to have the best life I can while I'm here. How to help the people I know have the best life, and my animals have the best life . . ."

I cleared a big lump from my throat but still could barely speak above a whisper. "One of the reasons it was so devastating was because I can't help feeling that I utterly failed him. I mean that's the ultimate to have it end in death, at least in part, I think, because of my mistakes. In that way, I think I was trying to play God and have it all work out just because I willed it."

Andrew softened. "I don't think it's that you were trying to play God so much as that you can't accept that you're human. You can't forgive yourself because you can't save everything. You can't make everything work out."

I couldn't talk anymore so I just nodded in agreement in the hope of ending the conversation. Then I feigned fatigue and went upstairs. Kiera got up and walked in unison with me up the steps.

Andrew wasn't going to let me off that easy. He followed me into our bedroom a short time later. "Maybe you need to get away for a while."

He stood waiting for a response or a reaction.

I finally answered, "Yeah, I think I do."

○

This all took place leading up to that cool September night, every-thing I've written up to now. The night Andrew had this conversation with me. The night the coyotes called. The night that Kiera paced and whined to be set free. The night that I lay with her on the floor.

I didn't need Andrew to point out that I was in a serious tailspin. I knew I had to pull my life back together and find a way to come to grips with all of the changes and losses that had happened over the last few years.

○

It was close to one o'clock in the morning. The coyotes had quieted. Kiera had finally fallen back into a sound sleep by my side. I'd tried, but been unsuccessful at getting back to sleep. I got up, went to the computer, and booked myself a flight to Montana.

CHAPTER 13

Montana

SOMETIMES YOU TAKE a trip because you're running away from something. Sometimes you take a trip because you feel there's someplace you need to go. And sometimes you take a trip because your soul is crying out to you, and you don't know what else to do.

I was heading to Montana. I didn't know why I felt I needed to go to there; I just knew that I did. It wasn't a place I'd ever gone to before, or even really knew much about. There was just something inside me telling me that's where I needed to go. I figured I'd find out why once I got there.

What I did know was that it was time for me to figure out how to shake myself free from the pervasive despondency that had swallowed me since losing Magic; it was time for me to figure out how to claim back my life. I also knew that Andrew understood this was something he couldn't help me with; this was something I had to do by myself.

○

I pressed my face against the plane's window to better survey the mottled colors of fall amid the checkerboard patterns of fields and hills below. Seeing the land from this perspective triggered a memory of a conversation that had stuck with me since college.

It was with a girl who'd roomed next to me. She was an army brat who'd moved nearly as many times as she was years old, until her family had finally settled on the plains out west, which she'd come to love. We were talking about the different places we'd lived and traveled to. She suddenly became quiet as her eyes filled, before admitting how homesick she'd become — not so much for her family or friends, it turned out, but for the open spaces. Ultimately, she came to feel so claustrophobic in little hill-and-dale New England that she transferred to a college out west.

Back then, I couldn't imagine anyone not loving the cozy, hugging feeling of clustered towns, windy roads, and hilly, treed countryside. But now I viscerally understood what she'd been talking about. Even though I'd never been on the plains, I'd developed that same kind of need. The craving for open spaces was one of the irresistible urges pulling at me. I was feeling desperate to be able to see far without obstacles or barriers — without buildings, trees, hills, or even bends in the road blocking my view.

To see so far . . . How that had defined my life for decades. To see so far, so I could plan, protect, anticipate. Where did that all come from? In reflection, I realized this was something that had happened long ago, when I was quite young, maybe even as young as five, when I got my first Sheltie. That's when I'd first set myself up as protector, guardian, helper to those I loved. To say that I identified with the qualities of that dog wouldn't be a stretch. I took my job every bit as seriously as she did. These were some of my most identifying characteristics. Conveniently, I'd always had well-oiled instincts to help me see far, to sense the shifts in the coming tides. Except for the last few years, when I'd felt as blind and disoriented as any newborn pup.

Perhaps even more crippling, I felt that I'd lost my ability to see with faith and optimism. I'd come to anticipate problems instead of solutions, hardship instead of ease. A simple and telling example: Just driving to the airport that morning, I'd imagined getting stuck in traffic, delayed at the check-through—plotting how I'd meet each challenge, instead of expecting an easy drive and a relaxed departure, which was what had actually happened.

It wasn't that I didn't have faith; it was a cinch to have faith and optimism and encouragement—for everyone else. Because I could help them. But there was no help for me. I'd have to do it all myself. And I thought this even though there were many people around me who would have gladly helped in a second, if it had ever occurred to me to ask. I just never got good at asking.

I would make this part of my mission—to find some kind of faith in life again, to embrace faith, to have the kind of bone-deep faith Andrew had. And to accept that needing help wasn't a weakness or a failing, rather, just part of being human.

○

As soon as I stepped out of Billings Airport, I got hit with a blast of wind that blew a smile across my face. Right away, I felt spectacularly alive and euphoric, with a great sense of adventure.

I tossed my small duffel bag onto the passenger seat of the rented SUV and turned onto Highway 90, going west. The state speed limit was a liberating seventy-five miles an hour. There were hardly any cars on the road, even at evening rush hour. If this had been Albany, I'd have been crawling in bumper-to-bumper traffic.

With enough light left to take in the sweeping vistas, my head swiveled around like an old hoot owl. I was drunk on the magnitude of space. The feeling that enveloped me wasn't exactly one of coming home; it was more of a sense of rightness. Flying down the highway, I zipped up my down parka and opened all the windows, feeling free as a bird.

An hour and a half later, in Big Timber, after a total of fourteen hours of travel, I turned onto the dirt drive just as the light began to fade. I found Sally, the proprietor of the Carriage House Bed and Breakfast, at the office around the side. She was a trim handsome woman, with bobbed strawberry-blond hair. As we stood at the door ready to go to my room, her other guest for the evening arrived. I immediately liked this woman, Michelle. She was about my age and also traveling alone. After brief introductions, we proceeded over to a tastefully refurbished turn-of-the-twentieth-century carriage house nestled by a creek and cradled by the mountains.

After a tour of the house, Sally stayed for a while and graciously fielded questions about how she'd come to Montana. She recounted how she'd recently left an executive position at a very successful software company to live out her dream of getting away from it all and owning a B&B.

After Sally left for the main house, I decided to go for a walk. I needed to get outside and stretch after being cooped up in planes and cars all day. In the pitch dark, I was immediately accosted by several large bodies bounding across the road in front of me. From the sight of white flags bobbing in retreat, I knew they were a bunch of deer. This unexpected surprise flooded me with adrenaline, so I trotted for about a quarter mile to burn off the nervous energy. Then I stopped and listened to the quiet. It was so very quiet—as though a blanket had been thrown over the earth and it had peacefully gone to sleep.

I slowly circled around to take in the 360-degree view. The night was ink black, making it hard to tell where the stars sprinkled overhead ended and the twinkles of light from ranches spread miles apart began. It was as if I were standing in the middle of infinity.

Looking up at the vastness, I thought about Andrew and the difference between his journey and mine. It seemed that his was more about people, more about working out his connection to his heart. He had the faith thing down. I had the heart thing down and needed to work on faith. Maybe that was one of the reasons we made such a good fit; we knew how to help raise each other up.

And I thought about Cait and how she was already becoming a perfectionist at such a young age—as I had. I wanted to help her learn how to loosen her grip on trying so hard to make everything work out just right.

I'd come to Montana knowing I needed to resolve my issues, my connection to my spiritual life, as seen through nature, as seen through the universe and wide-open spaces. I needed to find a way to stop being angry at God. Then again, I thought maybe my problem with faith had nothing to do with God. Maybe being angry at God was an entirely separate matter. Maybe my problem with faith was really as simple as having lost faith in myself.

I went back to the house, grabbed Michelle, and dragged her back out with me. This night sky was too magnificent not to be shared. I don't know how long we stood outside looking up, but it was long enough for us to share our life stories, as well as give ourselves sore necks. As it turned out, we had an uncanny amount in common, not least of which was the recent loss of a dog.

Later, reading the guest book in my room, I was struck by how nearly everyone, in one way or another, had written about having come to this place as a seeker. I wondered, as I reached over to turn out the light, how many had found what they'd come looking for. As I buried myself deep under the piles of covers, I heard coyotes singing in the distance. I smiled and drifted off to sleep.

◯

The clock read 6:10 a.m. I'd been up since four. My body was still on Eastern Time. So I did the only reasonable thing I could think of to pass the time until breakfast: I went for a walk and greeted the early-morning daylight.

The sun had just crested over the rugged peaks of the Crazy Mountains, which dramatically rimmed the back of the property. I got my first good look at where I was. In the foreground there were hundreds of acres of open plains. Behind me were some buttes that I'd been warned not to climb because of rattlesnakes. I set off down the dirt road I'd started on the night before. Deer and antelope were scattered across the fields. A herd of cattle was grazing in the far distance. It was all quite a sight to behold.

No one knows for sure how the Crazy Mountains got their name, but one legend has it that a woman was driven crazy after her family had been killed. She'd supposedly wandered into the mountains and lived out the rest of her days alone there. I wondered if there was something about these mountains that attracted "crazy" women—crazy in need of faith, crazy in need of healing, or crazy for adventure and feeling alive. I guessed that Sally, Michelle, and I all fit this bill. But then I decided the lives of three women whose paths had briefly crossed weren't enough from which to draw any conclusions. Still, I couldn't help but speculate, at least about my own connection to the Crazies.

For the past week, in my preparations for the trip, I'd had moments when I'd thought it was a simple matter of needing to escape the struggles of my life for a while. Certainly I needed to escape my dreary thinking. I thought at other times it was the accumulated sadness I wanted to run from.

So much of that sadness was embodied in having had to kill Magic.

When friends asked what happened, I wasn't capable of speaking about it, so I'd just mumble how Magic had developed complications from Lyme disease, and I had to have him put to sleep.

Put to sleep . . . much too polite a code name for what it really was. It was killing, plain and simple. It didn't matter to me that I wasn't the one who gave the injection; that was an incidental detail. I had killed a dog that I had loved with all my might. I had killed Magic.

Killed Magic . . . Yes, that's what had gradually been happening over the last few years—the magic I once felt in my life, the magic I once used to so easily be able to capture, had slowly been killed off.

Maybe somewhere I was thinking that if I could rehabilitate Magic—help him have a life that fit his name—I'd be rehabilitating something in me. A sense of passion and purpose, of feeling alive. Well, we all know the end of that story. Just naming a dog *Magic* doesn't bestow him with any. And just wanting magic to be part of a life doesn't automatically conjure any.

I'd woken up from a dream that morning that seemed to provide at least part of the answer. My father, my brother Rip, and I were at our childhood house. I was about eleven. We were working in the yard, pruning an old apple tree. A branch snapped back and hit Rip hard in the chest. It caused his heart to start fibrillating. He said he knew he'd developed a blood clot. I told him to get to the hospital and have his Coumadin level checked. He didn't want to be bothered. My father boomed out, "Don't endure what's wrong with your life! Change it!" And then I woke up.

It seemed a dangerous blow had happened to the heart. I guessed I'd better figure out how to take better care of these matters of the heart. And to stop enduring and start learning not only how to change, but how to create a life that offered healing, offered the possibility of magic again.

Maybe over the course of the week I'd find that I might have to do a lot of crying so I could empty myself out and have room to breathe again, but mostly the feeling I was having was that I was really happy here, and that I wanted to have fun. I wanted to take the long road home. I wanted to stop at places, instead of rushing from one point to another. I wanted to let the land seep into my bones.

○

Back on the road, my only task for the day was to decide whether I was going to Yellowstone or Glacier. I'd have several hundred fewer miles of driving if I chose Yellowstone. And there was the very real possibility that I could get all the way to Glacier Park and not be able to drive through because of snow shutting down the mountain passes. It would be a race against the clock.

But from the time I'd seriously considered making this trip, I'd felt that I needed to travel to the Going-to-the-Sun Road in Glacier, which had been described as one of the most beautiful drives in the world.

That thought was compelling enough. Then there was the story about Sun Mountain (which the road is named after). In one of the Blackfeet origination stories, there was a tale about an old Blackfeet chief named Napi. He'd created the world and then the Blackfeet tribe. When he'd grown old, and done all he could to give his tribe the best life he knew how, his work was done. He went to the top of Sun Mountain, and traveled on to the next world.

I was feeling that I needed to send the worn-out part of me on to the next world, too. If Sun Mountain was a portal, maybe that was the place where I could do it. Of course, I had no idea how I could make that happen. I just knew that it was a place I needed to go.

Within forty-five minutes, I'd reached the turnoff that would have taken me to Yellowstone. I found myself waving to it as I sped by. Going-to-the-Sun Road and I had a date. I'd just have to have faith that it'd still be open all the way through by the time I got there.

But within two minutes I'd fished out my cell phone and dialed Glacier Park Information to find out the current road status. I reckoned I was going to have a fair amount of work to do on this faith thing.

○

I had a few days of driving ahead of me, which left me plenty of time to think. I traveled through landscape surreal in beauty, and incomprehensible in expanse. This was a place where miles lost meaning, and time seemed both to stand still and move at light speed.

Oddly, I found it extremely difficult to hold many thoughts while traveling through this otherworldly terrain. I was so caught up with each moment, so unable to string one moment to another, that there didn't seem to be enough room in my brain for anything other than what my eyes were seeing right then.

And right then, what they saw was a bald eagle swooping down from a butte and over my car to the other side of the road, where it effortlessly snatched a trout out of the river. I pulled over and got out to watch it feast. It was exhilarating to have this opportunity to watch this great bird in its natural state, doing what it was intended to do. I felt very lucky.

I felt my father's presence as soon as I got back into the car. I couldn't help but smile. I was glad someone was there to share this experience with me. Really, I'd felt his presence on and off since I'd landed in Billings, and in no small measure, I'm sure this was why I was able to travel with such a feeling of absolute adventure, without a trace of fear. I knew my dad was, in some way, right there looking out for me.

○

Two days later, I stood across from Sun Mountain. I'd made it. The rapidly shifting clouds scudded across its peaks like sailboats racing in a regatta. I pulled my jacket tighter and searched its jagged face and scalloped ridges, looking . . .

Looking for what?

Looking for Napi to magically appear? Looking for a secret portal to open? Looking for a way that I could give away to the Sun all my sorrows and burdens?

Earlier that morning, I'd been the only car driving into the west entrance of Glacier. The man in the booth confirmed that Going-to-the Sun Road was open all the way through — all fifty-two spectacular miles. I was grateful to have the nearly deserted park so much to myself, so I didn't have to feel self-conscious about my compulsive need to stop to touch and smell the earth; to rub my hands in the dirt and on the rocks, to feel the roughness of the tree bark on my skin, to sniff the grass and taste the air. I'd been feeling for so long that I'd been looking at the world without really being in it, like it was in a museum diorama behind a glass enclosure that I'd come to observe. I now so desperately wanted to be in it, to feel a part of it once more.

I noticed a distinct drop in temperature as I started the climb through steep, tightly packed, rugged mountains sloping precipitously into thickly forested valleys. In some ways, it didn't look all that much different from parts of the High Peaks of the Adirondacks. But the feeling was very different. It was as though with each turn of the road I was spiraling up to Heaven. As much as the views of the valleys below were compelling, I needed to look up.

By noontime, I'd made it to Sun Mountain. I was sure it was Sun because there was a sign with an arrow pointing right at it. I pulled as far over onto the shoulder of the road as I could, got out, and climbed up a ways. I folded my arms tightly over my chest, trying to keep away the cold whips of wind. The sun was to my back shining on the face of the mountain, lighting it up in high relief. It looked like it'd be a hard mountain to get to the top of.

"Okay, Napi, how'd you make it up there, if you were ever a real person to begin with?" I muttered under my breath. I continued to scan the mountain's face, looking for a probable place where this Napi character would have picked to catapult himself into the next world.

By now, the wind had blown most of the clouds away, revealing a cerulean blue sky. The sunlight weaved across the mountain, stopping momentarily to rest on one of the scooped-out peaks that directly faced the sun. As I watched the light play, I noticed that this one scooped section of the peak looked like two hands carved into the mountain, palms cupped and facing up, like they were trying to capture the rays of the sun in their fingertips.

I decided that's where I would have climbed if I'd been Napi. It seemed like the perfect spot to be transported into the next world. Then I turned to face what he would have been looking out over. I was able to find a line through the trees where the sun shone on my face unobstructed. I immediately felt several degrees warmer.

I wasn't sure what I needed to do to release myself from the accumulated sadness that had overtaken my life, to send it all on to the next world. I pulled my wool beret down over my ears and stuffed my cold hands into my pockets. I leaned against the side of a rock outcrop that acted as a shelter from the wind. And then I did something I hadn't done in years. I talked to God. I asked to be released from all the sorrows that had saturated me for so long.

In that moment, it all seemed too much. Too much that I had gotten on a plane by myself, to go all the way across the country, to be here freezing on a mountainside, thinking that a simple little chat with God would resolve all my problems, would carry away the pains of my youth, and the struggles and losses of my adulthood. Hot tears streamed down my cheeks.

I took a deep breath and kept my eyes closed and face upturned to the sun, feeling very unsteady. I gave myself a pep talk: "This is what you came to do. Let yourself do it."

I began to whisper once more. And whisper, and whisper.

I whispered to be free of the remnants of my youth, when I decided the way to get love was to be valued for being helpful and trouble-free. When I expressed few needs and gave of myself until there was hardly anything left to give. When I insecurely waited for someone to tell me I was doing a good job, that I was a good person, and that I didn't have to do any more. When I wanted someone to rescue me from myself, the way I tried to rescue everyone and everything else.

I whispered my longing to be free of the unbearable pain of missing my father, of helping Andrew get through the loss of his mother and father, of helping him start a new business with all its attendant worries and struggles. And of all the ignorant mistakes I'd made with all of my animals over the years that I believed, in the end, may have cost Magic his life.

I whispered until I finally stood quiet. Finally emptied.

After standing there for quite a while, I was thinking there was nothing more to do or say; it was time to go. But I really didn't want to go. There was no place I had to rush to. There was nobody waiting for me. I was free to stand there through the night if that's what I wanted to do.

I started to think about time, and how I'd become its prisoner over the years. I was always trying to figure out how to plan for the future; worrying if there was a future to plan for; feeling trapped by the responsibilities and details of what had to be done in each day, leaving not enough time for joy or play.

I had an overwhelming urge to empty my pockets, to throw away everything I didn't need right that second—no matter what it was. I wanted to start traveling light through life again, as I once had long ago.

I stuck my hands into my pockets, ready to jettison whatever they grasped. I apprehensively reached in, felt around, and burst out into a fit of laughter. It was too perfect. The only object I had on me was a pocket watch on a chain that I'd bought a few weeks earlier. With Cait in first grade, I'd needed a watch to know what time I signed her out of her after-school playgroup, and I hated wearing wristwatches. It was a cheap knockoff with a large face so I could see the numbers without my glasses.

I balled it up and sent it sailing down into the valley below, catching the glint of the sun. I felt a giddy sense of freedom as I watched it fly.

I stood there for a long while with nothing but the sound of the wind at my back and the sun on my face. I felt so light that I was sure if I spread my arms I could fly.

It was in that moment that I knew how Napi did it. I knew how he made it to the next world. He had unburdened himself so fully, had made himself so light, that his ecstasy lifted him. The sun showed him the way, and the wind blew him there.

I got back in my car and started down the mountain. Winding carefully around the curves of the deserted road, I felt my father's presence especially strongly.

"Let it out," I heard my father say in my head.

I thought I'd just done that. What more was there to let out? Then it was as if somebody opened my jaws with a wrench and held my mouth open. Out came a succession of involuntary bloodcurdling screams. I couldn't stop. They just kept coming and coming. I began sobbing uncontrollably. I didn't know if I was sobbing because the sound of the screaming was so pitiable and had scared me so badly, or because I couldn't believe I had such raw and ragged pain stored in my body.

I pulled over and dropped my head on the steering wheel, my body racked with sadness. After a long while, the tears were spent. I was exhausted from crying, and light-headed from hyperventilating. I knew my sadness was finally spent. I'd done what I'd come to do. In the comfort of that realization, I fell asleep.

When I awoke, the sun was hanging low in the sky. I felt tired but exquisitely light and happy. And I felt whole.

Before leaving the park, I wanted to take a hike with the last of daylight. I set my sights on a small plateau just beyond one of the alpine meadows. Walking out in the fresh air gave me a chance to sort out what had happened.

It didn't take a scientist to determine that recent events had pushed me under, and that I'd started to drown. I'd recognized that I had to find a way to break out, to get free and surface for air — for me.

I needed space, wide-open vistas, no obstacles, no asks, no needs except for my own. For too long, I'd been doing what I'd tried to do as kid. Trying to take care of everything and everyone; trying to keep them all safe and together. I had to accept that this was an unreasonable expectation, and that, really, no one expected this of me except me. It was time to let that all go. I could do the best I could do, and I'd have to let that be enough.

I also realized that I'd gotten into the habit of letting my father be the only one I'd let help me; the only one I felt comfortable reaching out to and taking anything from. I'd have to learn to let other people begin to fill in this void. I came to see that it was the only way I could start letting go of my father. And that letting go didn't mean losing him. If anything, it meant that I could better keep my heart open to better hear him whenever he whispered in my ear.

And I finally realized that I was the only one who could free me — could give me permission to take care of myself and to live my life as I needed. I realized that even if someone else had tried to do any of those things for me, I would still have remained a prisoner, because I was the only one with the key that would unlock the door. Like Dorothy, I'd had the power to get home to myself all along.

Montana had been tugging on me for a long time, and I hadn't known why. Sitting on the edge of that plateau, looking out over the immense grandeur of it all, I finally understood why. Montana was a place that put everything back into the proper perspective. The human was not the significant object on the landscape; it was the vastness of the landscape itself. Out here, without distractions and clutter, it was so easy to see what mattered. What mattered? Me and God.

Montana was a place where I could let everything unimportant fall away; I could see as far as I needed, and know that I would be okay. Here was a place where I could remember, I could know, that God so clearly rules and I could only humbly follow the course of my destiny.

Walking back down the meadow, catching the first stars twinkling through the night canopy, I smiled at the simplicity of my destiny in that moment. Hunger pangs reminded me that I hadn't eaten since breakfast, and the dark pushed me on to find a place to sleep.

My last day in Montana served up another beautiful day. I'd be using it to make the eight-hour drive back to the airport.

During those first early-morning hours, my thoughts turned to Kiera and how much I'd been missing her. I reflected on the extraordinary journey she and I had shared, and how much her presence meant in my life. I smiled at our habit of always checking for where the other one was, no matter where we were or what we were doing—as though this simple knowing that the other one was right there somehow helped make the world a better place.

And I thought about how I'd tried to do for Kiera what I'd done with all my great loves—as I'd certainly done with Andrew and Cait—I'd tried to do everything in my power to make her life as good as it could possibly be. I'd been sure that getting another dog would be the very thing that would lift her life to perfection. Looking back now, how painfully ironic.

Having provided myself the distance (physically and emotionally) to look at all that had happened, I came to see how Kiera had shown me over and over that while she'd accept whatever I put in her life, all she'd ever wanted was me. Any and every chance she got, no matter what dogs or people were around, it was me she sought out. It was me she needed to be near and spend time with. It was me she wanted to come back to.

It felt freeing to fully understand that neither one of us needed anything outside of ourselves to complete what we had. That didn't mean that we had a need to shut anybody else out, or that we wouldn't welcome the opportunity to share what we had. It was just that now it was finally okay for me to accept that I didn't need to add anything more to make Kiera's life better. If I chose to, I'd be clear from now on that I was doing it for my own needs and not for hers.

As much as thoughts of Andrew and Cait were drawing me home, Kiera's call was equally strong.

As the sun lifted itself up over the horizon, I found myself traveling through an expanse of land that transported me to a place of emptiness. A place where there were no people, no cars, no houses—and no man-made sounds. Beckoned by a dirt road that disappeared into the vanishing point, I drove to an isolated spot. I got out and walked, hearing nothing but the crunch of gravel underfoot. Overhead, there were no jet trails—only clear blue skies. At first, I could hear the subtle song of the wind. Eventually, even the wind died down, and I heard absolutely nothing. I stood still, soaking up the land, and merging with the silence.

At other times in my life when I'd faced emptiness, I'd been scared and intimidated by it. I'd viewed it as a hole filled with loss and loneliness. This morning, it was the other kind of hole I was looking into; this emptiness felt very whole—pregnant with possibilities and potentials and whatever dreams I wanted to give to it.

I beheld a panoramic view that spread out before me; I could see for what felt like hundreds of miles. For the first time in years, it seemed, all the pieces were falling into place and I could finally take a deep breath.

I don't know how long I walked, or how long I stood out there. It didn't matter. I was in a place that had been special-ordered for me, and I wasn't in any hurry to leave it. Any last remnants of tension drained away, leaching into the ground under my feet. And I could feel the beginnings of something new being born in me. So new, I had no idea what it was. Except that I was aware that it was something good.

I'd come to Montana hoping to find healing, hoping to find some answers. I'd been generously handed everything I'd come looking for. I'd made my peace. I knew that I could finally accept things for what they were, instead of what I wanted them to be.

I was ready to turn my car and my heart toward home.

PART 5

The Road Home

CHAPTER 14

Unfinished Business

I BARELY GOT through the door before my happily howling dog was leaping all over me. Caitlin, not far behind, flung herself up into my arms from a standing broad jump over Kiera's wriggling body. She looked as though she'd grown an inch in just one short week. Andrew smiled and stood patiently waiting his turn. I finally peeled off my two little barnacles and made my way over to my husband. I hugged onto him, breathed in his familiar smell, and held on tightly. In the midst of this wonderful mayhem, from the corner of my eye, I caught sight of a few piles of stuff I'd been meaning to put away before I'd left. I was home. But more importantly, I was happy to be home.

I also came back to work to the great news that we'd won another significant account that would decisively push us over the top. We finally felt that the business had taken off and we could fly at cruising altitude.

There was only one more piece of unfinished business I needed to take care of; one more thing I needed to face to make things right. That unfinished business was Kiera.

I'd been noticing that since Magic had died, Kiera had started taking over as aggressive protector. She'd started to develop some bad habits that needed to be dealt with pronto. I'd already had two strikes because of aggression problems. This time I had to hit a home run.

○

Suzanne Clothier was a well-known and well-respected trainer whose book, *Bones Would Rain from the Sky*, I'd just finished reading. (Having developed a habit of reading dog training books over the last year, I found a curious comfort in continuing to read them.) Suzanne's book exuded a deep understanding of dogs, as well as a great humor, not to mention a training philosophy that embodied everything I was striving for. I couldn't believe my luck when I discovered from her Web site that she didn't live far from me, and that she was available for private training sessions.

It was time to get unstuck from what had been my *Incoming! Duck and cover!* mode. I couldn't afford the luxury of wallowing over Magic's loss any longer. I e-mailed Suzanne shortly after I got back, briefly describing Kiera's training history and current behavioral issues. I concluded with a request for an appointment. She e-mailed back to say she had an opening in two weeks. I took it. "No time like the present" was going to be my new mantra.

○

I have this thing about being on time; it's something I inherited from my father. So I was relieved when I still managed to arrive punctually at Suzanne's farm, after having gone on an unexpected sightseeing tour resulting from a wrong turn.

Suzanne was waiting outside for me at her training area. She was the kind of person who looked you straight in the eye to take your full measure. While she was quick to smile, joke, and laugh, she was also very much about the business at hand. She reminded me of me, so it was easy to feel comfortable with her.

We got right to work. She asked about Kiera's history. I explained that maybe she'd think my concerns with Kiera were nothing more than typical Aussie behaviors, but that there was a backstory that would give the fuller picture. I shared Kiera's and my travails with Molly and Magic, and brought her up to date with where things stood now.

I outlined my goals: I wanted to work on helping Kiera be more relaxed about letting people onto our property and into our house. That meant no bumping or rushing at people. I explained that she'd also become somewhat dog-aggressive over the last year, and I wanted to get that under control. And I wanted to improve how she responded to distractions when we were out for a run or a walk, so that she wasn't always at the ready to charge off and do battle. Ultimately, my goal was to be able to take her anywhere and have her remain calm and in control, and therefore be safe.

Kiera decided she liked Suzanne right away, too. All it took was for Suzanne to sit with a big hunk of freeze-dried liver in front of her, from which she'd break off little bits that she'd toss to Kiera after she'd complied with Suzanne's directions. Suzanne was looking to see how Kiera worked.

As Suzanne and I began talking, the liver bits stopped flowing. Kiera, dismayed with this new development, started running through every trick in the book, hoping Suzanne would be impressed enough to give her another bit. As we continued to talk, Suzanne tried to keep a straight face while Kiera went through her circus act, posthaste. She kept upping the ante: a paw, both paws, a sit, backing up, coming, lying down, sitting up, standing up on hind legs, jumping up, head on knee, speaking, being quiet. I swear, if there had been a tightrope there, Kiera would have figured out how to walk across it, to see if that would get Suzanne to feed her.

Still Suzanne offered her nothing. Kiera looked truly befuddled. She knew she was performing brilliantly. Why wasn't this woman rewarding her? She stopped for a second to survey Suzanne with an intense gaze. I could see the gears in her brain shift; she'd come up with another idea. Now with each rotation through her tricks, she increased the speed with which she did them. I guess she thought the sheer blizzard of behaviors would be enough to bedazzle. By this time, Suzanne was cracking up. I tried not to laugh because I didn't want to encourage Kiera.

Suzanne, in a very calm voice, finally explained, "Kiera, that's all very special, but I haven't asked you to do anything yet. You only get food when I ask you to do something and then you do it."

Kiera cocked her head and came in closer to rest her head momentarily on Suzanne's knee, as though considering this point. Suzanne took pity on Kiera and asked her to sit. Kiera sat so fast I couldn't be sure she had ever been standing. Suzanne gave her a reward, and a big "Good Girl." Then Kiera was finally able to relax. Suzanne lazily scratched Kiera's scruff.

Suzanne looked over at me and continued talking. "Well, there's no problem with Kiera wanting to work, and that's good for training." Then she chuckled to herself and said, "Ya know, there wouldn't be any Middle East problems if we could assemble all the Kieras of the world and send them over, because these guys are brilliant negotiators. You say, 'Here's the price for this' and she goes, 'Okay, how about this instead?' So you've got to see everything as a price tag where you say, 'Look, you want me to throw your ball or Frisbee? This is what it's going to cost you.' You've got to make her work harder."

Suzanne possessed a remarkable ability for translating everything from the dog's experience to its human equivalent. She continued, "Remember how when Cait learned to write her first letter, you were like, 'Wow, great!' When she's eighteen and writing, you won't be saying, 'Wow, that's amazing!' Or when was the last time someone really complimented you on writing a check—great job. It's not about the dog just needing to sit as a nice way of saying 'please.' Sometimes 'please' is not actually sufficient. The smarter the dog, the stronger the expectation has to be. Asking Kiera to sit is like asking Bill Gates for a hundred dollars. It's just not meaningful. She does it with half her brain tied behind her back. She sits and then she's asking, 'How about "Down," how about this? Let me show you something really cool. What do you think about that?' She's just making up her own rules."

I had to laugh because it was so true. Part of the problem was definitely that Kiera was too damn smart. It wasn't always easy to know how to focus and channel all that intelligence.

I finally confessed, "I don't really think Kiera's the problem. I think I've been the problem; I got so blown away by all the events with Magic that I've pretty much lost all my confidence. I'm at a point where I feel insecure and second-guess everything I'm doing. I'm the one who needs the training. I need you to teach me how to get it right, so I can teach Kiera how to get it right."

Suzanne reflected thoughtfully, "Some of this I think is co-incidental. I think the fact that Magic was acting the way he did, which is sad to say, probably couldn't have come at a worse time for Kiera, but he didn't cause it. These tendencies are already here with her." She paused and smiled. "And if you're half as smart as your dog, we'll get this all turned around."

Then she launched into an hour of intense nonstop, eye-opening instruction. She suggested we go on a little stroll around her property, where the *Ahas* came fast and furious. Every two feet we walked, there was another distraction for me to handle with Kiera: dogs, cows, horses, chickens, pigs. Suzanne started by instructing me to reward Kiera with lots of treats and praise anytime she voluntarily looked at me and away from a distraction. Kiera would see a new distraction, and bark and lunge. I would calmly call her name and each time she looked, as soon as she looked, we'd have another big party with lots more treats and praise. It didn't take long before Kiera's first impulse upon seeing another distraction was to immediately look at me. This was work that would lay the foundation for Kiera and me to begin rebuilding our connection to each other.

Suzanne watched me while I watched Kiera, giving me feedback, guiding my hands on the leash, bringing me back into focus when I started drifting, telling me what to say and what to do when. With the help of such clear coaching, I began to feel some of my old confidence knocking at the back door. It was exhilarating, and I felt unbelievably happy. I was being given the hope that I could become sure again of something I hadn't been sure of for a long time—that I could do this. And I could do it well.

I left Suzanne's place that day feeling that a fog was lifting from my head and from my heart. I left with more clarity about dogs and training than I'd gotten from all those dozens of books I'd read. There's just nothing like having someone standing by your side to show you the ropes. Kiera and I went home with a specific plan for practice.

○

Suzanne prescribed a course of action that included working with Kiera by taking her for walks in town. This was all part of strengthening the quality of Kiera's and my relationship. We would start back at the most basic level with how Kiera walked on a leash with me. As Suzanne explained, "Sometimes you have to back way up, right to the beginning, where the root of a problem lies, and take it from the top." I was to make sure that we didn't pull each other, because, as Suzanne also explained, it takes two to pull. Whenever the leash got tight, I was to give Kiera a gentle tug and then release all tension. And if I had to, I should tease her with play, by running back a few steps to get her refocused and reengaged with me. I was to practice being aware in each moment that I was with Kiera, "while gently and persistently shifting the balance toward one of mutual agreement and cooperation." This would also help Kiera to remember to truly be with me when we were together.

My work included paying attention to the earliest signs of anything that aroused Kiera, and then show her how I wanted her to behave. At the first indication—an ear flicked forward, eyes widening or hardening, body becoming rigid—I would step in, and using my hands to guide her body into different positions, I would gently reshape her body language into a more relaxed pose. This simple technique worked miracles. After a few trips into town, I could see a noticeable difference in how Kiera and I related. She was starting to look to me for what we needed to do next, instead of making unilateral decisions. She was no longer feeling that her job was to stay on constant red alert.

On one of those afternoons, as Kiera and I did some laps around the blocks, I found myself becoming obsessed with watching other people and their dogs—watching for those tell-tale signs of a dog in trouble. I found myself developing a sense of great caution with dogs—a caution that I never had before. In the old days, I'd never have thought twice about walking up to any dog, unless it was obviously indicating that it wanted me to stay away. I'd since realized that most people weren't really skilled enough to make that assessment with any dog. There were too many subtle cues in a dog's communication that most people would never pick up—where they might (or might not) see something the dog was trying to relay and not understand what it was they were seeing.

I'd always told Cait not to extend a hand to a dog unless she had first asked permission from the owner, and I'd discourage her from approaching any dog she didn't know, but now I was adamant about it. I became wary of anyone's assessment of and ability to recognize the truth about their own dogs. I started noticing how common it was for people to be in varying degrees of ignorant bliss or denial about their dogs.

I was never one of those people who thought dogs were people in fur. Now I fully understood just how much they were not people in fur. Only a couple of circumstances needed to line up to send them back to being more like their coyote relatives than to the Lassies and Rin Tin Tins of the world. I read that in any given year, the number of reported dog bites hovers around one million. It was the second most likely injury for children during the summer months—a sobering statistic.

I worried that Cait might develop a fear of dogs from having witnessed the aggression problems with both Molly and Magic, but she hadn't. If anything, it seemed to have helped her develop more confidence. I'd like to think I could take some credit for this because of the way I handled those situations, but I think it's really just Cait's nature to be made stronger by the challenges thrown at her.

It wasn't that I'd become afraid of dogs, as much as it was that I'd learned to give dogs a healthy respect that, previously, I was somewhat cavalier about. My situations with Molly and Magic had forced me to learn way more about dogs than I ever thought I wanted to know. The upside was that it forced me to become a more responsible and aware dog person. Still, sometimes this was of little comfort. Especially when Kiera would go to the spot where Magic was buried and lie with him for hours at a time.

I couldn't help remembering a conversation with a friend back when things were at their worst right after Magic died. This friend had been bold enough to suggest that it was all for the best. He felt little compassion and mostly annoyance for my plight with Magic, and did nothing to hide his view. His sentiment was that people go through a lot worse, and that, on the whole, I'd made a mountain out of a molehill. Putting Magic down was the right thing to do, he thought, and the only question was, why hadn't I done it sooner and just moved on.

I could have tried to justify myself, but I didn't. Given the challenges this guy faced in his life, I completely understood where he was coming from. There was that and the fact that our human-centered culture doesn't really allow acknowledgment or condone admission of just how deeply animals can work their way into our hearts, and above all how painful it can be when we lose them. And anyway, this friend only spoke out loud what some of my other friends secretly thought. I knew that. And I also knew that they didn't remember who Magic was before the changes started happening, or for that matter never saw how wonderful he was when it was just Kiera, him, and me alone. It would have been a waste of time to try to explain to anyone what drove me to keep trying. There weren't really any words that came close to capturing how I felt about Magic or how much I loved him. Nor were there any words to describe how awful it was to lose him in the way that I did. Only another person whose life was so intertwined with animals might know, and with that person there was no need to explain.

○

It was time for another shot in the arm from Suzanne. She agreed to meet me in town on a summer day, which would provide us with hordes of people, unpredictable encounters with dogs, swiftly moving traffic, and running children — in short, all the boisterous and chaotic commotion our town had to offer during the height of tourist season.

We met at the park and camped out on the bench across from the carousel. From this vantage point we were afforded the full gamut of potential triggers for Kiera without having to hike around town. Kiera sat and leaned against my leg, not quite sure what to make of this place. To her, it seemed a cornucopia of confusion.

Suzanne and I chatted for a while about what Kiera and I'd been up to, all the while keeping an eye on and working with Kiera whenever she became tense. As usual, Suzanne focused more on what I was doing (or rather on what I wasn't remembering to do) while correcting and educating. Suzanne was one of those people who emanated a presence that I just felt good being around. The slight downside was that I found her very wry and observant sense of humor so funny that it was sometimes hard for me to remember to concentrate on what was at hand because I was too busy laughing. It was a small price I was happy to pay.

Just as I was sharing with Suzanne my realization about how few people, even so-called dog people, knew how to behave around dogs, a young woman saw Kiera and started heading straight for her with hand extended. As she approached, I looked right at her and, in a polite but loud voice, explained that Kiera was in training, and I'd appreciate it if she'd not try to touch her. The woman smiled and kept walking up to Kiera. Kiera started to feel anxious and backed up a little. Again, I told the woman I did not want her to pet Kiera. She kept coming. I was stupefied. It was like something out of a Fellini movie.

Finally, Suzanne shoved her arm forward, motioning for the woman to stop in her tracks, saying, "Do not pet this dog!" And the woman finally registered that she was being told no and veered away. I watched her talking to her friend as they walked on. Her face and body language suggested that she felt embarrassed and hurt for being shooed away when all she wanted to do was pet a dog. But there had been no time to explain to her that she was putting herself, and therefore all of us, into a potentially difficult situation. Kiera jumped up on me, putting her paws around my neck to give me a hug and a lick, as though to say, *Whew, thanks. That was a close one.*

Suzanne decided it was a good time to get on the move, so we collected our stuff and started walking up to the main street. The sidewalks were packed with people. Suzanne continued to observe and instruct while keeping a "weather eye" to everything around us. I was looking down at Kiera while we walked. From her vantage point, it must have seemed as though we were trying to wind our way through a forest of legs.

We were doing great. I was staying focused. Kiera was staying relaxed. The leash (something I'd come to think of as our umbilical cord rather than a ball and chain) was loose. The rest of the world could have dropped away in that instant and Kiera and I wouldn't have cared. We were in that perfect moment; that perfect dance between two beings who were completely connected to and understood by the other. Something in my heart started unlocking as I remembered and drank in this buried feeling. Kiera and I were discovering magic again.

While still in this state, I heard Suzanne warn me that a big dog, dragging his owner behind him, was lunging for Kiera. In a perfectly seamless sequence, she moved in to block the dog and tell the owner to get it under control while I negotiated Kiera back and away, and over against a storefront where I kept her shielded until the dog and owner were past. Kiera had a moment where she got ready to defend herself, but when she realized that she was being taken care of, that she was safe with me, she saw that she didn't need to. After it was all over, she looked up at me for direction. I told her, *Let's go*. Happy that I had a plan so that she didn't need one, we trotted to catch up to where Suzanne had been left standing after running interference for us. She offered a hale and hearty "Good job!" Kiera and I smiled.

Suzanne continued to prove an extraordinary teacher and leader as the afternoon wore on. I couldn't help but contrast the difference between how tense I'd felt on those days in town when it had just been Kiera and me versus how relaxed and easy it was to do the same things with Suzanne there. Because I knew I could rely totally on Suzanne's confidence and leadership skills, I was provided the space to do one job — concentrate on

Kiera. I didn't have to think about anything else, as I would have if it had been Kiera and me alone. By not having to do Suzanne's job *and* my job, I didn't feel crazy, as though I had to watch and manage every little thing around us all by myself. And that was a huge relief. I could actually relax and enjoy doing my job because I knew I had a good leader who knew how to do her job.

Seeing how at ease Kiera was, I realized that this was what Kiera was now experiencing with me. And I understood in all of my being what this meant for her. I wanted her to know this feeling all the time. It was as if Kiera and I were walking together inside a bubble that neither one of us wanted to leave. I knew this was how it was supposed to be. Not that the rest of the world was shut out. It was exactly the opposite. Kiera and I were finally and again sharing the same world together. I vowed that I would become the kind of leader for Kiera that Suzanne was modeling for me.

I don't think I could ever come close to Suzanne's flair for people–dog metaphors, but if I had to come up with one that described what I thought had been occurring since I started this new work with Kiera, it would be: Kiera was no different than a latchkey kid who'd been left to her own devices, because she had a mother who was sometimes physically absent and often mentally distracted. From lack of parental guidance, Kiera grew in independence and, for survival, began making decisions on her own—some good, some bad. When the mother finally decides to reinsert herself after one too many crises, the kid doesn't remember how to rely on the mom anymore because too much trust has been lost. Over the last few weeks, Kiera and I had come a long way in rebuilding that trust. It was starting to show.

○

Kiera nudged me and yipped to let me know it was time for our walk. No matter what the weather, she knew we'd go. This day we walked out into a cooling sun shower. I never tired of being out in the fresh air with my beloved girl. As she rhythmically trotted along in front of me, I watched her through a shimmering mist rising off the hot pavement.

I started ruminating; before Kiera, Molly, and Magic, I'd been one of those dog people who'd been lucky enough to wind up with easy, even-tempered dogs who practically trained themselves. I'd been allowed to mistakenly believe that my well-behaved and "safe" dogs were a result of my superior knowledge and training skills. After all, I'd worked for a veterinarian for a few years, and had read a few books on dog training. What more credentials did I need to appoint myself an expert?

And I was oh so quick to judge other dog people with unruly, ill-behaved, or aggressive dogs. Because, when all was said and done, how hard was it to put in the time to do it right?

How hard indeed.

My journey with my dogs had brought me into a world I could have scarcely imagined—a world full of remarkable love and staggering pain.

I would not trade this experience. All of that love filled me with a spiritual wholeness, and a willingness and desire to keep trying, even when it became crushingly hard. And all of that pain forced me to keep learning and keep looking for the answers. Until I finally grasped, in my core, what it all was: the extraordinary and profound role that dogs play in my life.

Enveloped by the quiet surrounding us, I felt touched by something sacred. I became aware of a funny kind of shift taking place in me.

For some reason, a story about a Buddhist teacher and student popped into my head. The story went like this: A student went to his teacher and asked how he, the student, could find his Buddha nature. As Buddhist teachers are wont to do, the teacher replied rather tersely, "You have no Buddha nature."

The student went away, thought about that, and came back to ask if dogs have Buddha nature. The teacher answered, "Yes, dogs have Buddha nature." The student then asked, "If a dog has Buddha nature, then why don't I?" To which the teacher replied, "Because you have to ask."

Looking at Kiera, as she so perfectly existed in her world, it struck me that she did indeed have Buddha nature. Like the student, I was always one to ask.

The cooler temperature agreed with Kiera, so she was especially playful. She started rushing out, twirling around, and bounding back, trying to get me to play tag with her, which snapped me out of my reverie. I cut into one of the fields where Kiera could safely run off-leash.

At the sound of the clip coming off, she did a standing leap, bouncing up to plant a big lick on my cheek, before she tore off to get some of her crazies out. Watching her zoom around filled me with complete joy, as if it were me doing the zooming. She'd do a couple of laps running like a total maniac. Then she'd realize she hadn't checked in for a few minutes, and she'd come dashing back, sometimes skidding into a nice sit right in front of me, sometimes leaping into my arms, the weight of her finally knocking me over. She took advantage of my prone position, jumped right on top of me straddling my body, and licked and yipped at me until I was laughing so hard tears streamed down my cheeks.

It was if she were saying, *Get up, you lazy bones, and play with me!*

Lying there in the rain with Kiera's breath on my face, looking into her eyes, I understood completely my connection to her. It was one of those rare moments when it all becomes perfectly clear. When you go somewhere for that split second, and you understand everything in a flash before it all closes back in around normal reality.

This thing I had with Kiera—with all my dogs over the years—went beyond unconditional love, and beyond companionship. It was about the oneness everyone looks for: oneness with the self, oneness with something outside the self, and oneness with a greater being. It was all of these things, and it was more than these things.

In that moment, I completely merged with Kiera and everything around me. I was Kiera, I was the trees, I was the falling rain—and they were all me. I was experiencing the quantum connection, the spiritual connection of all things. I was experiencing, in that quick sweet moment, that separation is illusion, and oneness the reality.

In that moment, I understood how Kiera knew when to go wait at the door long before she could hear my car coming down the road. I knew now how she was able to sense my feelings without a word. And I understood why I was no more able to ignore her feelings, wants, and needs, any more than she could have ignored mine; these things went beyond just being sensitively tuned to each other.

In that moment, I knew what it was I saw in her eyes every time she looked at me. There was some part of her that was directly wired to me. Was me. We were both part of the greater All That Is. She lived daily and hourly the experience of union that I was only beginning to grasp on a deeper experiential level, though I'd been working on this for years.

Some people find God through church, others through love, others through sports, art, music, service, and on and on. I realized that I found my connection to God through nature and my animals. It was a pure state for me where everything was so clear and simple.

Knowing this filled me with an indescribable joy. I got Kiera, I got me, and I got Kiera and me in one fell swoop. And that was a mighty powerful awakening; one that I didn't think I'd be quick to lose again.

I began to feel that if I didn't move my heart would burst with this knowing. So I finally pushed Kiera off, did my own version of a doggy play bow, and took off with her in hot pursuit. She'd let me get out a ways and then come speeding past, blowing my doors in. She'd wheel around, slowing down, as though she was going to let me catch her. As soon as I got anywhere near close, she'd leap in the air doing a 360 and be off again. We played like this until dark, as only two enlightened beings—or lunatics—can.

CHAPTER 15

Finding Kiera

KIERA CONTINUED TO make steady progress with the occasional setback here and there. And Suzanne continued to play a supporting role. But there was still a piece of Kiera that worried me; there was still a kind of wild intensity about her that wouldn't necessarily be obvious to anyone else but me. I could see it in her eyes. One of the ways it sometimes showed up was that no matter how much exercise she'd get—even running nonstop several miles a day—she'd still need to tear around the yard at breakneck speeds. She couldn't just turn off and relax.

I was seriously considering checking in with the town running group that met in the park to see if anyone training for a marathon was interested in a running buddy, when serendipitously I got a flyer in the mail that Theresa, Kiera's instructor from puppy obedience, was offering a beginning agility class. The last time I'd considered doing this with Kiera, she'd been too young. And then the idea got lost in the shuffle with all the craziness that ensued. This seemed like the perfect time to take the class. I had no doubt that the more and different ways I could find to keep training Kiera, the more stimulated and therefore, interestingly enough, the more calm she would be. I signed up.

Thankfully, the class turned out to be small. There were only four other dogs and people in the group. If there were any dominant dogs in the class, I knew Kiera would move quickly to defend herself (something I believed was left over from the Molly days), so I hurriedly scanned the ring as we entered, looking for telling signs. There was a nervous terrier (a possible problem), a big goofy Poodle (no problem), a sweet perky Sheltie (no problem), and a very intense Ainu (a Japanese Spitz breed and almost certainly a problem). I kept my eye on the Ainu.

I was surprised to see not even one Border Collie in the group. Not that a specific breed had agility cornered, but, except for the Sheltie, these wouldn't be dogs I'd necessarily expect to see on a course. I'd find out later that some of the other owners had the same idea I had: They saw this as an opportunity to get more training to help with their difficult dogs. A few enviable souls had come for the mere fun of it.

As Kiera and I walked over to get into line, the Ainu rushed at Kiera. Her owner was ready and had her checked before she could make contact. Kiera stiffened, ready to engage, but was able to keep walking when I called her on. We moved off to the side to keep a safe distance from the group. I exhaled a silent *phew*. Theresa offered introductions and began the class.

I couldn't believe how much fun it was. Kiera and I had a blast. Chaining all the steps to get through an obstacle was a breeze for Kiera; she caught on like flash paper. (Of course, there were plenty of treats proffered as incentives—rocket fuel for my rocket dog.) With each obstacle we learned, it was as if she were saying, *Great! Piece of cake. What's next?* She had a hard time waiting her turn. Every time Theresa would call out a name for someone else to go next, Kiera would stand up. She was ready, wiggling her butt, boring her eyes into Theresa, chanting in doggy language, *Pick me, pick me. Oh, oh. Please pick me—me, me, me!* None of this was lost on Theresa; she knew how to keep a dog's incentive up. She actually did let Kiera go a couple of times in a row once.

The first few classes were all structured the same; with our dogs on leashes, we'd review the obstacles we'd learned the week before and learn a couple more. We'd covered the A-frame, the chute, the fence, the tunnel, the dog walk (a narrow plank high off the ground), and the tire jump. We just had a few more obstacles to go and then we'd be concentrating on putting them all together. Finally, Theresa informed us that eventually we'd be expected to get through the whole course with the dog off-leash. At this news, my chest tightened and I broke out in a clammy sweat. I'd never before let Kiera off-leash when there was a mix of strange dogs and people around.

Theresa also suggested that we come on our own to get in extra practice time. I was definitely going to take her up on that. If I expected Kiera to get through this without going after the Ainu or an unanticipated, loud and clapping bystander, I had my work cut out for me.

○

It was a bright, star-filled night; Cait was asleep and Kiera was resting at my feet, exhausted from all the day's exercise. Andrew and I had gone to sit outside on our deck that overlooked our pond. It had been almost a year since Magic died; we both felt that we were getting far enough away from the epicenter of the blast to be able to reflect on what had happened.

Andrew wondered if I had come to any clearer insight as to what had caused my undoing. We talked further about some of the experiences and realizations I'd had in Montana, and continued to have since then.

At one point Kiera jumped up on me, nosing and licking my face, as she always did whenever I expressed a hint of a distressed feeling. I pulled her onto my lap.

Andrew said, "What struck me about the whole thing is that I never would have guessed it was that bad for you back then until the very end. I know I was at work when you were dealing with most of it, and I know you tried to explain how overwhelmed you felt at different times, but it never really made sense to me because you seemed so capable—like you always knew what you were doing."

I replied, "Yeah, but that doesn't have anything to do with having it together or standing on a strong foundation. That just has to do with the ability to do what needs to be done in the moment. You could be a total nut and still do what needs to be done in the moment."

"So you were faking it?"

"No. I just have an instinctive ability to respond to the moment," I said. "The problem is that when you appear competent to other people, it doesn't occur to anybody to comment that, 'Oh, your pants are on fire, did you know?' They'd assume that of course you'd know that your pants are on fire. And you don't know."

Andrew smiled and nodded. Then he shifted forward in his seat and asked, "I've always wondered . . . Why do you think Kiera came back? I mean, don't people usually have the view of reincarnation as progress? If somebody reincarnates to come back for you, isn't everything supposed to be better?"

"I don't know . . . Who's to say it isn't better the way it's worked out?" Then I asked Andrew, "Why? Were you thinking that we were brought back together so we could complete this great love and that's the be-all, end-all?"

"Well, yeah."

"That's not why she came back. It was never an issue of completing the love. The love can't be any more complete than it was. It's always been complete. It's been about having another experience. It's about taking the relationship of having a dog in my life to a whole other level of intensity and awareness."

By this time, Kiera had settled herself down in my arms. I rearranged her body across my lap to shift her weight to a more comfortable position. Andrew smiled. "She's pretty big to be a lapdog." Then he reached over to scratch her head. "You know that my feelings about Kiera run deep. And I recognize that the other side of the coin is that by the nature of having someone like her in our life, there's also an intensity to the relationship that is to be valued greatly. Precisely because she's not some simple being; she's very much alert, very much there. All of that is part of it. That doesn't stop me from wishing that she was also easy. And maybe by the time she's eight or nine we'll have both."

"I think she's already much easier, and I expect her to continue to get easier. But as to a trade-off . . . I'm not sure," I said. "I'll probably always wonder. I think Kiera could have been a different dog if I had gotten her alone and we didn't go down the road we went."

"The other thing that I realized yesterday when I picked Cait up from her friend's house and met their new dog," Andrew said, "is that that dog's owner would have no idea how, in that moment, when I was talking with her about whether her dog was friendly, that I saw the last three years of my life flash before me . . ." Andrew's voice cracked. Then he laughed weakly. "You can see how far we've come from the epicenter."

I laughed anemically, too. "I think, in a way, what would be hard for someone to understand about this experience unless they've been through it is that it's sort of like what some of my immigrant friends talk about having gone through by leaving a country that's familiar and known. You travel to a place you've never been before and you have to start over again. There's a piece of you that never fully recovers from journey, from the things you've left behind. It changes you and you can never go back to where people live with their docile Golden Retrievers."

We'd also just been through a couple of weeks where we'd heard from several people we knew who'd had to have their old or sick dogs put to sleep.

Andrew said, "I asked Tim how they were doing, and he said they were putting on a brave face. He said the last two days were just so horrendous and sad. He said, 'I'm not even going to go into it.' And I was thinking, *You don't have to. Been there. Know it all too well.*"

We laughed and sniffled at the same time. Then Andrew said, "I was joking the other day with somebody about one of my grandmother's favorite expressions, 'If you live long enough, you see everything.' It's incredibly, powerfully, frighteningly true. And that includes all of these terribly sad, incredibly difficult experiences. It's all part of the mix . . ."

He paused and smiled. "And then there's you. You get to find your dog twice—or should we count three times—in one life."

○

I closed the gate securely behind us before I let Kiera off the leash. She looked up at me for an indication of where we were going to start.

Kiera and I had been spending a lot of afternoons after work and before it was time to pick up Cait from school running around the agility course. When it was just her and me like this, we were magic in motion. She sailed around and over everything as though she were floating on air.

I snapped on my treat pouch, surveyed the course, and plotted the run in my head. Kiera, getting impatient, pawed at my pant leg as though she were trying to get this car out of park and press on the accelerator. I reached down, scratched her head, and took off for our first obstacle. Kiera flew over the jump and then looked at me to find out where we were going next: the A-frame or the chute. I pointed. She slung through the curved chute like a boomerang and shot through the tire jump without breaking her stride. I was ready to give her a treat for a great performance so far when she blew past me to the gate, barking and lunging at the fence, as another classmate showed up with her dog. I heaved a sigh and went to get the leash. More work to be done. Always more work to be done.

I needed to change my tack. Kiera had the agility part down. Practicing it was fun, but it wasn't getting at the heart of what Kiera really needed to learn—how to tolerate distractions and other dogs being around. As my father used to say, you have to take your opportunities where you find them. As I looked up to open the gate to let the other person in and get Kiera out, I saw my opportunity.

Theresa also ran a doggy day care center on site. We'd have to pass a dozen or so barking dogs enclosed in a chain-link yard to get to our car. Previously, to get back and forth to the agility ring, I'd get some treats out, get Kiera focused on me, and then we'd gallop through this doggy gauntlet. This time, my plan was to stroll casually and calmly—well, casually—back to the car. As I expected, all the dogs raced over and barked at the fence in keyed up, shrill voices. Before Kiera had a chance to rush over to take all of them on single-handedly, I sat her down and gently reshaped her body posture. I laid her ears down, I patted her scruff down, and I sat her back so her weight was over her haunches instead of on her front legs.

It worked. She could sit there calmly while the other dogs barked. A shower of treats. A few more steps. The same drill all over again. Until we finally made it to the car. Then we walked back to the ring. Back to the car. Back to the ring. By the end of several passes, Kiera was content to stay focused on me and walk calmly past all the dogs—for that day.

○

On the next to the last class, I asked Theresa if I could run Kiera off-leash while the other dogs remained on leash to see what would happen. She suggested I let a short leash hang on Kiera so that if there were any problems we'd have something safely to grab her by. I thought my heart was going to pound out of my chest as I dropped the leash.

Kiera immediately tensed. She was ready. But ready for what? I was never so focused on her, trying to discern every minute muscle movement, read every facial tic. Was she getting ready to bolt at the Ainu? I called her on before she had a chance to do too much thinking. Her face relaxed into her version of a smile as we took off. She couldn't have cared less about the Ainu; she wanted to have some fun.

We were halfway through the course when Kiera got me laughing so hard I was doubled over. Either she wasn't happy with how she'd gone over the dog walk or she liked doing it so much that she sent herself back to go over it again. I was already running on to the next obstacle and it took me a second to realize that she had backtracked. Then she started looking around for me, trying to figure out where I was. We were like a couple of Keystone Cops run amok. We wouldn't have won any ribbons with our performance that day, but we sure did have fun.

On the way home, I was figuring out how many more practice runs we could get in before the big day—our last class where we'd run the whole course with the dogs off-leash. Maybe ten, if we were lucky. I hoped it would be enough.

○

The day of our final class was breezy with a sky full of billowy clouds. The trees were swaying, rustling loudly in the wind. I wondered how this would factor in for my motion-sensitive dog. We were walking calmly past the fenced dogs when I stopped in my tracks. Kiera looked up at me, wondering why we'd stopped. She hadn't seen them yet.

Surrounding the agility course were a couple of troops of Girl Scouts who'd come to watch. I took a deep breath and gave myself a pep talk: "This is not a problem; Kiera will be fine if you are fine. Remember, it's the quality of the connection you create between the two of you." Just then, Kiera caught sight of the girls and started to lunge.

But it wasn't the crowd. She'd spotted a dog friend that she wanted to get over to greet. Once she was allowed to say her hellos, she walked nicely past everyone and in through the gate.

We were slated to go last so we stepped off to the side to wait. Every once in a while, Kiera would whip her head around at a noisily swaying tree branch or an especially loud cheer from the crowd, but otherwise she was pretty mellow. Fortunately, with such a small class, we didn't have to wait long for our turn.

"Okay, girl," I leaned over and whispered in her ear, "this is your big day. Let's go have some fun!"

When I clicked off her leash, she leapt up in agreement and planted a lick on my cheek, then whirled around to look for the first obstacle. We were off. The sounds of the wind and the crowd dropped away as Kiera and I ran with an invisible cord between us. We were flying in a world of our own making, with eyes only for each other. Over the first dog walk, over the fence, tight back in to make it up and over the A-frame, around to the tunnel, through the tire jump, onto the wait table, up and over another dog walk, over another two fences, through the chute, and down the weave poles to the finish. Everyone cheered with appreciation. Kiera did a standing 360 to second that motion.

CHAPTER 16

May the Circle Be Unbroken

I RUSHED INTO the house, stripping off my gear as I went. Kiera raced past me into the kitchen and skidded into a sit in front of the closet where I kept her dog food. It was her way of reminding me that it was her dinnertime. I didn't need to look at the clock for confirmation; her stomach kept better time than any clock in the house. But I hadn't hurried into the house for that; I'd run for the phone. I had momentous news to share.

"Andrew, she did it! She did it!" I was laughing and out of breath.

"Who did what?" he asked.

I could visualize him sitting at his desk with the receiver tucked between his ear and shoulder while he continued working away on the computer.

"Kiera. She did it! She finished the whole course with no mistakes."

"Awesome."

"That's not the half of it!" I rushed to tell the rest of the story. "There were other people and dogs inside the ring waiting their turn. And there were people lined up all along the fence outside, and she didn't even bat an eye. I let her off the leash and walked her up to the starting obstacle and we were off. She took off so fast I thought I was going to have a heart attack trying to keep up with her. But she made a clean run. A clean run!" I was jumping up and down with excitement.

Andrew was silent with appreciation. He knew what this news really meant. It meant that she didn't try to attack any dog, or rush and bump any people, or allow herself to get distracted by any onlookers cheering or yelling. She stayed focused and self-disciplined. She had crossed the Rubicon; I knew she was going to be all right now. That didn't mean that I could relax or rest on my laurels, but I knew that she was safe — safe from the fate of Molly and Magic. She had made it.

Andrew offered his heartfelt congratulations and said that he'd be home in a while. Cait was at a friend's, and it was still light out. I was still flying high from Kiera's victory and wanted more time outside with her, alone together. Her dinner would have to wait. I had other plans.

After she tracked the direction of my gaze to anticipate my intent, she bolted to the front door and jumped up, trying to paw her leash off the coat rack. When she couldn't get the loop over the hook by herself, she whirled around to me on her back legs doing a jig. I laughed.

"Yes, my girl" — I caught her front legs and tussled her head — "we're going."

I barely got her leash snapped on before she'd opened the front door to head out to the road. She started down our well-worn path, a road that we'd walked down together more times than could be counted. It was a beautiful, sunny fall day, the air was brisk, and my girl and I were glad to be together out in it. It'd been quite a ride, and I was so thankful she was still here by my side.

We'd walked about a half a mile; the sun was low but on our faces. I was deep in thought when I noticed that Kiera had come to an abrupt halt. Not all that unusual on one of our walks. She was always stopping to sniff the invisible trail left by those who'd gone before. When she didn't seem to have any interest in moving on as I reached her, I noticed how rigid she held her body as she peered into the brush along the side of the road. She didn't try to rush at whatever she was seeing, and she didn't bark. That was unusual.

Within a few steps, I was at the spot upon which she seemed fixed. I perused the bushes and saw nothing. I called her on as I kept walking. She reluctantly came. We passed the opening into the field at the other end of the overgrown hedges. Kiera detoured back and tried to pull me in. When I wasn't quick to follow, she trotted back to me and then, whining, trotted back into the field. Something had intensely captured her interest, so I decided to walk in and see if I could locate what it was. I was always on the lookout for wildlife, so what was a little detour?

Again, Kiera was rigid, tightly wagging, head high in the air, sniffing. This was behavior she'd offer when she'd caught the scent of a favored dog she was excited to see, just before she'd be ready to bound off and play. I looked again, thinking maybe our neighbor's yellow Lab was running free this afternoon, as he sometimes did. This would explain Kiera's behavior, since they'd become pals over the course of our many walks. The Lab was nowhere to be seen. There were no dogs, or any other wildlife in the field that I could detect. I felt a momentary flush of nervousness.

I was debating whether we should turn around and go back. It was late in the afternoon, getting toward dusk, and I didn't want to be out walking in the dark with coyotes around. I was pretty sure they wouldn't bother us, but I also didn't want to test that judgment.

Kiera started straining against her leash, heading toward the back of the field. It took all my strength with my heels dug in, leaning toward the road, not to get dragged along behind her. I was starting to get a rope burn on my hands and tried to wind the leash around my waist. There was no way I was going to traipse back into the woods, or even move as far as those fifteen-foot white pines dotting the field just ahead. Perfect place for an ambush.

Now I really just wanted to get out of this field and go home. Kiera's behavior, the diminishing light, and my own imagination were causing the hairs on the back of my neck to stand.

I was using all my strength with a heave-ho motion to pull Kiera around, and I was worried about hurting her neck. I finally decided to just pick her up and carry her back to the road. As I swung around to grab her, there they were — all six of them, silently standing in full view, not more than twenty-five feet away.

"Holy shit," I murmured as I sucked in a deep breath and slowly stood up straight.

Something about them gave the impression they were a family. I could easily make out the father as the largest coyote. He'd placed himself a bit in front of the others. He must have weighed fifty pounds and stood a little taller than Kiera. He had a beautiful gray and black-tipped coat. The mother was more fine-boned and a little more grayish tan in color. The pups looked almost full grown and were just starting to fill out with their winter coats.

Kiera's gaze was locked on the compact dark one on the end. She still had not barked. And everything about her demeanor suggested that she was not interested in attacking these animals. In fact, she seemed desperate to greet this scrawny guy she hadn't taken her eyes off. Nobody was moving a muscle, except Kiera, who was still straining at the end of her leash.

It took several long seconds to overcome my fright and collect my wits. Not knowing what else to do, I began wildly flapping my arms. "Shoo, shoo!" I yelled, feeling both scared and foolish. "Get outta here!"

Nobody moved. All animals remained riveted on each other.

I flung my arms again and rushed a few steps forward. The coyotes flinched but otherwise didn't budge. I finally picked up the biggest rock in sight and hurled it at the one that looked like the leader. It landed with a thud at his feet, sending up a little cough of dust. They finally broke ranks and scattered back into the woods. Kiera gave me the dirtiest look and let out a howl that for some reason instantly made me cry.

She howled again.

Unbelievably, the little scrawny one came trotting back alone.

He stopped several feet away, body relaxed, tail low and gently wagging. He looked at me, and then at Kiera. He play-bowed, stretched out his bowlegged back legs one at a time, and then started zigging and zagging at breakneck speeds, as though navigating an obstacle course only he could see. After he'd sprinted through his imaginary agility course, he began tracing wide arcing circles around us.

Something about him reminded me so much of Magic that, before I even knew what I was doing, I found myself kneeling down, putting my arms out and calling softly, "Come here, my boy . . ."

He stopped, looked at me, and hesitated.

Kiera, never one to miss an opportunity for escape, took advantage of my relaxed grip and made a run for it. She beelined over to him and they started licking each other's faces. I tried to sneak up behind her to grab the trailing leash. As I was about to fall on it, the little coyote took off, and Kiera was off like a shot racing right next to him. They were rolling and leaping over each other, and taking turns playing tag. They were in ecstatic play.

Meanwhile, I was in an unmitigated state of panic. I raced after them, thinking that if Kiera got her leash caught on something while she was running flat-out, she'd hang herself. I had no fear that the coyote wanted to hurt her, or lead her back to the pack. They stayed in open view and never once showed any signs of aggression.

I stumbled over a clump of dried hay and landed facedown. I couldn't believe this was happening. I knew there was no way Kiera was going to let me catch her. And the thought of anything happening to her was too devastating to contemplate. My legs felt as though they'd been shot full of lead. I couldn't make them work to stand up. I couldn't watch.

Sniveling in my sleeve, splayed flat out on my belly, I felt a scratching at my pant leg. I nearly jumped out of my skin, letting out a yelp. I had no idea if I'd snagged against a stick, or a field mouse had run over my ankle, or if Kiera had gotten tired and come back to me. I scrambled to an upright position, and was relieved to see she was walking toward me, sniffing at the ground as she came. When she got near enough, I lunged on the leash, threaded my arm through the loop, and wound the rest tightly around my wrist. She wasn't going anywhere.

She looked at me unapologetically, and then she stared straight past me. I swung around to see what she was looking at. It was the little coyote. There he stood for one last moment in the fading light, no more than an arm's length away, gazing up at me. He play-bowed and stretched out his back legs one more time, and then he trotted to the end of the field.

Stunned, I just stood there, with Kiera leaning against my leg as we watched the coyote recede. He turned and gave a final look, before slipping silently back into the woods.

EPILOGUE:

The Dogs of Dreamtime

IN THE DAYS that followed the encounter with the coyotes, I felt altered somehow. I became aware of a shift in my spiritual and emotional center of gravity. As though I were moving through a dream world—a time out of time, where, slowly, one realization after another began rolling over me, like ocean waves.

I came to realize that Magic had been given to me not so that he could live, but so that he could die. He had come to me so he could reach his freedom in a way that I could never have conceived. Of that, I felt sure.

And I had been given to Magic so he could bestow on me the greatest gift possible. His death was the catalyst that caused me to release a lifetime of grief. To empty myself so fully and push myself so far in that I was forced to find the missing pieces of who I really was.

I could see now that the Universe had had in mind a different happy ending for all of us. My need to try to control the outcome, to get to the happy ending I wanted—to have Magic be alive and with me—was keeping all of us in a state of suspended animation. I understood now that this ending was the right one.

I knew I had done the best I could do. I had to let that be enough and stop beating myself up. That was my great lesson in all of this: I had to learn to let go and trust that there was a bigger plan at work—bigger than I could imagine or begin to guess at. I had to have faith that there was a plan, even if I couldn't see it.

I believe there is a golden thread that runs through all of our lives. I'd temporarily lost sight of mine, and needed to learn to trust that it was still there. This is the purpose of faith, I've come to understand. It's the light that carries us safely through the darkness until we're able to see the light again for ourselves.

My Kiera was still here. She didn't run away with the coyotes; she came back to me of her own accord. I'd always had this worry in the back of my mind that her wildness would eventually take her away from me, too, as I believed Magic's wildness had taken him. And that, some night, if she could run off with the coyotes, she would.

Kiera, lying on my feet as always, looked up at me, as if reading my thoughts, and as if to say, *Don't you get it? My wildness is mine, not the coyotes'. I don't need to run off with them to be free, to be who I am. I have always been free. I have always been who I am. I've never left you and I never will. I'm still with you. I'm still here. And now finally so are you.*

Yes, I thought. Now finally so am I.

And I could see that it was I all along who had somehow been calling the coyotes to us. It was I who needed to meet these coyotes face-to-face, so I could stare into the face of my own wildness, my own need to stay connected to and be nourished by the natural world. And now, like Kiera, I could recognize these things inside myself. Because, in fact, I had been set free—free from my grief, and free from the fearful thinking that had been trapping me. I knew with certainty now that my freedom lived within me.

I'd been reminded of the unseen field behind everything that holds us all together. I knew I was still connected to Magic, and that he was still connected to me. And that I was one of the lucky ones, because I also knew how deeply I was connected to

Andrew and Caitlin. Like Kiera, this knowing was mine now and I knew what I needed to do to keep it healthy.

And, maybe most importantly, I came to understand that absolutely everything had happened for a purpose. Molly needed to get to Tara. Magic needed to get to his freedom. And I needed to get Kiera, to get Molly, to get Magic, to get Kiera again—to get me. It had been a harrowing journey, but in the end it was my dogs who had showed me the way home to myself.

I remembered a babysitter I'd had as a child who'd studied indigenous cultures and their creation stories—stories about how the world began. Knowing how much I loved my dog, she'd weave me magical stories about the aboriginal Dreamtime—the time before time—when dogs, she said, helped sing the world into existence and helped to create reality through their dreaming. Dogs had most surely played a key role in singing the world into existence for me.

I knew with certainty that these coyotes, along with Kiera, Molly, and Magic, had been my Dogs of Dreamtime. All of them had come from some ancient place deep inside me, with a story to tell that sang a part of me not yet fully born into existence. They represented archetypes, pieces of myself that needed healing, remembering, and strengthening. And each taught me much about the properties of time and dreaming—showing me how to bring into existence the world I wanted to live in.

Magic was my lost soul found. He came to me needy for love, needy for healing. He began his journey with me as a vulnerable, scared creature existing in a world that felt too big and beyond his control. I take comfort in knowing that, before his illness took him, he had discovered love, trust, and freedom. These were the very gifts he gave back to me. Because I knew time was his enemy, I worked mightily to dream a happy ending for him. I was shown that God is a bigger and better dreamer than I am.

Molly, whom I'd nicknamed the Unsinkable Molly Brown, was my courageous warrior. Some might have seen her deafness as a lack of wholeness. I never did. On the contrary, it allowed her to sweep aside distractions and stay intensely focused. Unflappable and headstrong, she'd brush off any opposition to her goal. She was no damsel in distress. She helped me remember my inner strength and fearlessness. For her, there was no time like the present. For her, I dreamed that I'd find the one person who would know how to honor her warrior spirit.

The coyotes were my storytellers. They shared their tales of wonder and awe. It was in how they revealed these old tales that summoned images, conjured realities, and changed my life when I was finally able to hear. They helped me remember that I had my own story to tell. They lived in a reality that did not include time. For the rest of my days, I will dream for them that they find a safe place in this world where they can live and play in peace.

And Kiera, my love . . . Kiera was my wise watcher. She never missed a thing and always seemed to know what it meant. She was my loving protector, vigilant and strong, patient and steady. She took her responsibility seriously and with sacred dedication.

She continues to remind me daily that just because life is uncontrollable and love cannot always protect and keep safe, this is no reason to stop living or loving. Time has been her friend. I dream for us that we will always find a way to keep coming back to each other so that together we can continue to brave the elements, go through thick and thin, and walk to the ends of the earth.

ACKNOWLEDGMENTS

WHEN I THINK of the people I need to thank for the existence of this book, they are all nearly equally important, for without any one of them there would be no book. I've listed them in order of turning points.

First up is my father, Robert J. Webster, who, among legacies too numerous to mention, instilled in me a love of dogs; along with my mother, Lillian, whose philosophy has always been a combination of, "The more, the merrier," and "Problem? What problem?" Two more wonderful parents do not exist.

Andrew, my true love, gets all the credit for teaching me how to write and for continuing to put up with my passion for my dogs. How I ever got so lucky as to nab him, I'll never know. Without him, I also wouldn't have Colin and McLean, each of whom is an inspiration to me. And then there's Cait, who is the light and joy of my life.

Cheryl Luciano, Theresa Richmond, Michele Wright, Bob Bellamy, and Suzanne Clothier helped me grow into a more competent and responsible dog person. Their much-needed advice and support has been invaluable.

Steve Lewis, Kathryn Shanley, Brian Shanley, Judy Webster, and Gina Karp cared enough about me to provide honest feedback and helpful suggestions.

Bob Silverstein believed enough in the story to take it on and represent me. He went way beyond the call of duty as agent, ultimately serving as tutor and friend.

Lorraine Welsh provided encouraging words at critical times of sagging morale, which kept me going to the finish line.

The people at The Lyons Press have all been outstanding to work with. Ann Treistman helped me plug up the holes, learn to tell time, and cut away the extraneous. I could not have asked for a more tactful, compassionate, and gifted editor. Jessie Shiers and Eliza Byron went the extra mile for me; Christine Duffy, Laura Jorstad, Kathryn Mennone, Gail Blackhall, Sharon Reid, and Michelle Brown comprised the rest of my very talented and supportive team.

First, last, and always, I have been blessed with all of my dogs—teachers of time, travelers of Dreamtime, where I'm sure we will all meet again.

RECOMMENDED READING

There are too many wonderful books to list them all. These are some of the books that helped me. Summaries are provided by Dogwise.com, which is also a great place to order your books.

Aggression in Dogs: Practical Management, Prevention & Behaviour Modification. Brenda Aloff.

Publisher: Brenda Aloff; 2002 Paperback, 418 pages.

For anyone who wants to know more about aggression or dog behavior. Learn how to avoid common mistakes that may promote aggression, build trust using positive reinforcement, and prepare for a long-term regimen to keep your dog safe.

Behavior Problems in Dogs. Bill Campbell.

Publisher: William E. Campbell; 1999 Paperback, 324 pages.

All veterinarians and most dog owners should have this one! Presents humane, efficient, and effective ways of dealing with negative behaviors. Third edition of a classic, extensively revised and updated with the latest concepts and techniques!

Bones Would Rain From the Sky: Deepening Our Relationships With Dogs. Suzanne Clothier.

Publisher: Warner Books; 2002 Hardcover, 320 pages.

Shows us how to find a deep connection with another being and to receive an incomparable gift: a profound, lifelong relationship with the dogs we love.

Cautious Canine. Patricia McConnell.

Publisher: Dog's Best Friend, Ltd.; 2005 Paperback, 30 pages.

How to help dogs conquer their fears with desensitization and counter conditioning. Step by step method can be used for any problem behavior that is motivated by fear—even for people!

Click for Joy! Melissa Alexander.

Publisher: Sunshine Books; 2003 Paperback, 200 pages.

*Won the Dog Writer's Association of America Award for Best Training & Behavior Book of 2003! Clear and accurate answers for over one hundred commonly asked questions about clicker training in one essential reference. Packed with information experienced trainers and newcomers alike can put to use immediately.

Clicking With Your Dog: Step-By-Step in Pictures. Peggy Tillman.

Publisher: Sunshine Books; 2000 Paperback, 200 pages.

The answer for all pet owners who want a dog to be a real partner and friend. Step-by-step illustrations explain the clicking process more clearly than ever before. Here's the pet-friendly way to teach your dog good manners and great tricks— without punishment or force.

Culture Clash. Jean Donaldson.

Publisher: James & Kenneth; 1996 Paperback, 221 pages.

Get rid of your dogs-are-like-humans thinking and learn to appreciate the *true* strengths and abilities of your canine companions. Find out what really makes a dog tick, what motivates him and how to get the behavior you are looking for!

Dog Language. Roger Abrantes.

Publisher: Dogwise Publishing; 1997 Paperback, 264 pages.

Why dogs do what they do and how we can express ourselves so our dogs can understand us better. Organized in alphabetical order and cross-referenced.

Don't Shoot the Dog. Karen Pryor.

Publisher: Bantam Books; 1999 Paperback, 188 pages.

Use behavioral training on people, dogs and other animals to make changes! End undesirable behavior; learn "affection training."

Excel-Erated Learning. Pamela Reid.

Publisher: James & Kenneth; 1996 Paperback, 172 pages.

Motivation, stages of learning, operant conditioning, factors that affect learning, negative punishment. In plain English—at last! Select the methods that work best for your dog!

On Talking Terms With Dogs: Calming Signals. Turid Rugaas.

Publisher: Hanalei Pets; 1997 Paperback, 33 pages.

Practical understanding of the dog's body language, especially signals used to maintain the social hierarchy and to resolve conflict within the pack.

Toolbox For Remodeling Your Problem Dog. Terry Ryan.

Publisher: Howell Book House; 1998 hardcover, 192 pages.

The Toolbox is a set of principles and practices you can use to analyze and address any behavior problem you may encounter. Unlike other problem-solving books that are limited in scope, Terry arms you with the tools you need to design your own solutions. Her method is based on positive motivation and rewards.

LYME AND OTHER TICK-BORNE DISEASES:
INFORMATION AND LINKS

Tick-borne disease is becoming epidemic in the United States. It's serious and, in some cases, it can be deadly. Lyme disease has now been reported in all forty-eight contiguous states, though cases are most heavily concentrated along the East Coast, California, and the north-central states.

There's a lot of confusing and conflicting information on the treatment of this disease. What follows is the most current information available to date (July 2006). It represents what I now do for my dogs. Everyone should discuss appropriate treatment with his or her vet.

THE LYME PERPETRATOR: DEER TICKS
The tiny deer ticks are the carriers of Lyme. Never going dormant, they remain active year-round and can transmit the disease at any time, though most cases are reported during the spring and fall. Because deer ticks are so tiny (the size of a sesame seed), they are very hard to spot on dogs. People often miss them on themselves as well. The nymphs, which are most often responsible for Lyme transmission, are even smaller than the adults.

SIGNS OF LYME
Lyme is a shape-shifter disease that carries a variety of bacteria. For this reason, signs of Lyme can vary. It can also present with all

kinds of weird signs or no signs at all. And different vets' knowledge may vary. One vet told me that dogs don't get Lyme's telltale bull's-eye rash. Kiera has had a few textbook-case bull's-eye rashes.

Many dogs who are positive will never show a sign. But the most common signs are arthritis, lameness, stiffness, joint swelling, soreness, lethargy, and fever. Often, people and dogs won't get bull's-eye rashes. In advanced cases, Lyme can cause kidney failure, heart problems, and neurological damage, which can lead to an aggression disorder. Because any of these signs, including lameness, can last less than twenty-four hours, if you notice anything different about your dogs, or they just don't seem right, even if you can't put your finger on it, please get them checked.

TREATMENT

The most accurate test now used in diagnosing Lyme disease in dogs (done at the vet's office) is the Canine SNAP 3Dx or the C6 SNAP test, which tests for C6 antibodies to Lyme disease and also tests for the additional tick-borne disease *Ehrlichia canis*, as well as for heartworm disease. The reason the SNAP test is so accurate is because the C6 antibodies are only present due to actual infection, not as a reaction to the vaccine, which is very helpful for dogs who have been vaccinated or whose vaccination status is unknown.

A positive on the C6 SNAP test requires a follow-up test called the Lyme Quantitative C6 Antibody Test. The C6 antibody test determines the level of Lyme (the titer) to find out if the dog needs to be treated with antibiotics. A dog with a titer over 30 gets Doxycycline and then is retested in six months to determine whether the titer has dropped.

There is also an annual vaccine. The first vaccine is followed by a booster in two weeks, and then a booster every year thereafter. The old vaccine did have problems. The new vaccine (Merial or Fort Dodge) is much safer, as it uses a killed virus as opposed to a modified live virus. Lyme-expert vets recommend the vaccine even for dogs who've had Lyme, if they live in endemic areas. The vaccine will help to prevent another serious reinfection. Some people question whether the vaccine will cause a dog to test positive. The answer is no; it's a different test—antibody versus antigen. Statistically, the risk of any vaccine reaction is less than one half of 1 percent.

I also use Frontline monthly throughout the entire year. You'll still find ticks when using Frontline, but it kills them within twenty-four hours of attachment. It's thought that the tick needs to be attached for more than twenty-four hours before the disease can be transmitted. Also, if you miss a tick, it will fall off the dog and look for a new host at its next meal. When you use Frontline, those ticks fall off dead. I include garlic in my dogs' food, which seems to repel ticks as well.

If one of my dogs does have a Lyme flare-up (both dogs are positive for Lyme), I immediately get them on a thirty-day course of Doxycycline (some vets recommend sixty days or longer, depending on the stage at which the disease is caught). Even if my dogs' signs resolve sooner—usually within a couple of days with treatment—I still give them the entire thirty-day course of antibiotics. The life cycle of the spirochete (the Lyme-causing bacteria) is thirty days. Without treatment or with shortened treatment, the infection can remain dormant before returning in the form of late-stage symptoms, such as neurological disorders, heart and kidney irregularities, and migrating joint pain. If the disease reaches this late stage undetected, it can be difficult to treat and is sometimes fatal.

It's important to raise people's awareness about the rapid spread of Lyme around many parts of the country because of the seriousness of the complications if left untreated. One of the expert vets on Lyme that I've gotten to know says, "When in doubt, test for Lyme."

TO BEGIN YOUR OWN RESEARCH

When you do an Internet search for "canine Lyme disease" or "Lyme disease + dog - human" or any variation on these, you'll hit the jackpot. I've included the links that I've found to be chock-full of information on their own, as well as providing many links to other terrific and helpful sites. Because there have been a lot of recent developments in the understanding and treatment of Lyme, I always check the page date to make sure that I'm reading the most current information. To do this, right click on the page and then click on Page Info.

http://saluqi.home.netcom.com/ticklinks.htm

www.minden.com/nowhereelse/canine_tick_disease.htm

www.idexx.com/animalhealth/laboratory/c6/index.jsp

www.caberfeidh.com/Lyme.htm

TICK-L LIST

If your dog has a tick-borne disease (TBD) or you suspect that he or she might be infected, consider joining the Tick-L. They are a knowledgeable and supportive group of people who've been through it. There are also vets on the list who are incredibly generous with help. To join, go to www.minden.com/nowhereelse/sub_on.htm.

Please visit my Web site, www.karenshanley.com, for more information or contact me at karen@karenshanley.com.